Just After

The Darlie Routier Story

By W.G. Davis

Copyright © 2021 by W.G. Davis

All rights reserved.

No part of this publication may be reproduced, distributed, or transmitted in any form or by any means, including photocopying, recording, or other electronic or mechanical methods, without the prior written permission of the publisher, except in the case of brief quotations embodied in critical reviews and certain other noncommercial uses permitted by copyright law.

ISBN: 9798734697009

I dedicate this book to Darlie Lynn Peck Routier

I hope that the words in this book will open people's eyes to these three truths.

You killed your two boys.

You staged the crime scene.

You deserve to be where you are today.

As of January 2021, there are six women on death row in Texas.

For the sake of justice for Damon and Devon Routier, hopefully, it will be down to five very soon.

In Memory of

Devon Rush Routier

June 14, 1989 - June 6, 1996

Damon Christian Routier

February 19, 1991- June 6, 1996

DEVON AND DAMON HOLDING HANDS
THROUGH LIFE AND INTO HEAVEN
NOW THEY ARE ANGELS PLAYING
TOGETHER

Prologue

I want to start by saying that the purpose of writing this book is not to disprove the statements that are being publicly shared by the Pro-Darlie camps. And it is not to support the statements that are being publicly shared by the Anti-Darlie camps.

Throughout this book, you will see where I tackle the misinformation that is being shared by both camps.

My goal is not to be 100% one-sided on sharing the facts and disproving the foolishness that is being shared as facts.

Over the years the Darlie Routier murder case has fascinated many people. This case has a cult following divided into three camps.

#1 the people who believe that Darlie is 100% innocent based on what they have read online or watched on television.

Sadly the online information is mainly based on the information that Darlie's family has released as fact to the public.

If you get the chance to sit down and read this information with an open mind you will see how ridiculous this information is.

Most of the information is real facts that are twisted to make the narrative match their belief that Darlie is innocent.

And to be honest, who would find fault in a mother or any family member at that trying to prove her daughter innocent of murdering her children.

However, people take that information and add an additional spin to the facts, and now it is impossible to read some of this information without laughing at the idiocy in these people's beliefs.

If you only rely on the pro-Darlie camp's version of the story, you will walk away believing that:

Darlie slept through the vicious killings of her two boys just feet away from her even though she couldn't sleep in her bed because the baby turning in his bed would wake her up at night.

Darlie was almost decapitated from her neck wound.

The bloody sock was a marathon's distance from the house.

The police never even questioned Darin regarding the death of his kids.

They believe that because the court reporter screwed up the transcripts that she never received a fair trial even though the jury physically viewed the evidence in the case.

They also claim that the jury never saw photos of her injuries even though the court documents clearly show that the wounds on her were presented in-depth to the jury.

They also claim that the jury ignored all of the physical evidence that contradicts Darlie's version of the facts and based their guilt solely on the video that shown her smiling and laughing as she sprayed *Silly String* on the graves in celebration, singing "Happy Birthday" to her son Devon on his 7th birthday just a week after the murders.

They also claim that the necklace on her neck saved her life.

Now the second camp is those who believe 100% that the police have arrested the right person and have taken the time to look at the facts of the case and ignore the ridiculous spins that are put on the story.

And then we have camp #3 who rely on the internet stories and comments and are so confused by what they have read that they sway from guilt to innocence like a playground swing in a tornado.

I want to clarify that I am in no way trying to distort any of the facts in this case to sway the reader one way or the other. As a former police officer myself, I will compare Darlie's version of the story against the physical evidence that the police found at the crime scene.

I will not use emotions or my personal feelings to try and sway you to believe one way or another.

And when you are done reading this book I will be confident that you will have read the facts of the case and compared them to the crime scene through an unbiased investigation of only the facts.

And one of the facts of this case was brought up in detail during the trial when Darin was testifying.

Question, "Would it be fair to say, that really back on June the 6th, by your version, we have got a real lucky intruder, don't we?"

Answer, "There was an intruder."

Question, "A lucky intruder?"

Answer, "Why lucky?"

Question, "I mean, after all, he picked a house where the window just happened to be open to the garage, right?"

Answer, "Yes, sir."

Question, "Just happened to pick a house where on that night, the alarm system is not turned on or armed, correct?"

Answer, "Yes, sir."

Question, "Lucky that in fact once he gets past the alarm system off, he gets through the window, open, when he gets to the utility room, he just happens to find a sock available to him for his use that night, right?"

Answer, "Yes, sir."

Question, "And lucky enough that when he does that, he gets into the kitchen and lo and behold there in the butcher block he finds a weapon to attack your two children and your wife, right?"

Answer, "My understanding is that it is called an opportunist."

Question, "No, my question is, he was lucky enough that evening, that once he got past all that, the murder weapon is actually provided inside the house; right?"

Answer, "Yes, sir."

Question, "Lucky enough that while he is attacking both your children, your wife doesn't wake up, right?"

Answer, "Yes, sir."

Question, "Lucky enough that after he attacks her, that in fact, she doesn't even get a good look at his face, right?"

Answer, "Yes, sir."

Question, "Lucky enough, that as he is leaving the house, he drops the knife on the floor there, and your wife doesn't pick it up and doesn't use it against him, right?"

Answer, "Yes, sir."

Question, "Lucky enough that when he gets into the garage that he doesn't deposit any blood on the floor, no blood on the window, correct?"

Answer, "I don't know anything about that."

Question, "And then lucky enough that when he leaves out that garage into your back yard, that he either scales that fence without leaving a mark, or he opens up that gate and he then latches and closes it without anybody detecting that either, right?"

Answer, "Yes, sir."

Question, "A real lucky guy, wasn't he?"

Answer, "Yeah, and I want him dead."

Question, "So do I. No further questions."

The Events Leading Up To a Nightmare

By all outward appearances, the Routiers seemed like a happy family living in an affluent suburb of Rowlett, Texas just twenty miles northeast of Dallas in 1996.

The Routier's seemed to have it all.

Darin and Darlie were married in August of 1988. They had their first son, Devon, just ten months later on June 14th, 1989.

Two years later on February 19th, 1991, their family grew with the birth of their second son, Damon followed by a third son named Drake, born in 1995.

The Routiers owned their own electronics company, called Testnec, which provided them with a comfortable lifestyle.

However, beginning in 1995, the company wasn't making as much money as it did in its earlier years. Even though the Routiers were far from broke their financial situation changed in the mid-90s.

The couple was having issues in their personal life too. The stress of dealing with vehicle issues and bills that had to be paid with limited income was starting to put pressure on the couple's relationship.

To top it off, they were denied a $5,000 loan from their bank due to their financial situation.

By June 1996, the Routiers had less than $2000 in the bank.

It was around this time that Darlie had been dealing with bouts of depression.

In May of 1996, Darlie wrote a suicide note to her children in her journal.

"I hope that one day you will forgive me for what I am about to do. My life has been such a hard fight for a long time, and I just cannot find the strength to keep fighting anymore. I love you three more than anything else in this world...I don't want you to see a miserable person every time you look at me. Your dad loves you all very much and I know in my heart he will take care of my babies. Please do not hate me or think in any way that this is your fault. It's just that I..."

Many people look at this suicide note and scream "OH MY GOD SHE MUST HAVE KILLED HER CHILDREN BECAUSE SHE WAS DEPRESSED!"

Depression affects many mothers. And I am not going to sit here and say that just because she contemplated suicide that she must have killed her children.

After she wrote this letter she called Darin and told him to come home.

When he arrived home she showed him the letter and together they cried and talked about the situation as husband and wife.

I will say that "Yes, Darlie was dealing with depression at the time that her children were murdered. And yes it could be a factor in the vents that lead up to that night."

Just over a month after Darlie wrote this entry in her journal contemplating suicide, another tragedy would befall the family.

A House of Love

We will use the statements made by both Darlie and Darin to the Rowlett police on June 8, 1996, (two days after the murders) Darlie's bail hearing on August 26, 1996, and testimony from Darlie's trial in January 1997 to put together the Routier's version of what happened on the night that Devon and Damon were murdered.

Whenever I find an inconsistency between the timeline that they give to the police and the statements that they made, I will notate them in the storyline.

Wednesday, June 5th, 1996

June 5th started like any other day in the Routier's home.

The two older boys rode their bikes with their friends until their father came home from work with their aunt Dana just after 6:00 pm.

At this time Darlie had a woman named Halina Czaban who had moved to the area just two months earlier working for her three days a week. She stated that she worked on Tuesday and Wednesday, and was suppose to work also on Friday of that week. She stated that she was paid $50 for three days.

She met Darlie because her daughter worked for Darin at his electronics company.

She said that she did the laundry, and if she had time, she would do some house cleaning.

She was also teaching Darlie how to cook some authentic polish meals.

Halina was also at the house on the previous day, Tuesday, June 4th doing laundry.

On Wednesday, June 5th she was doing laundry, but according to her testimony, "not so much."

After the laundry, she also dusted in the family room by the kitchen and vacuumed the downstairs of the home.

Halina stated that she had left the vacuum near the pantry door where it was normally kept after she finished up vacuuming.

We are going to point out the location of where Halina left the vacuum only to clarify some misinformation that the Anti-Darlie camp is saying about the vacuum cleaner location.

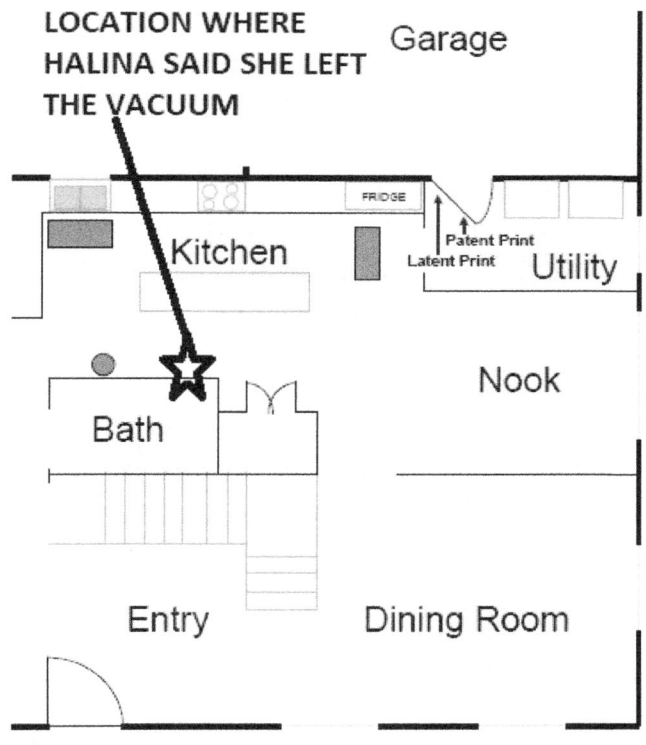

**The fact that Halina is the one who did the laundry in the Routier's home that week will play a big part later in the timeline.

Later that afternoon Darlie brought the jewelry box down from the second floor and showed Halina some of her jewelry.

This jewelry box was found by the police in the living room area of the home by the armchair where Halina stated that she had seen it that day. During the trial, it was identified as State's Exhibit 99-A

Halina testified that while Darlie was showing her the jewelry in the jewelry box she told her that she needed $10,000.00.

Halina also testified that Darlie's jewelry was already located on the kitchen counter area of the house between the kitchen and the living room.

She testified that Darlie asked her to bring the jewelry to her and after she looked at them she asked her to place them back on top of the kitchen counter where the police would discover them the next morning.

I added this fact about the jewelry on the counter because many people are saying that Darlie took off the jewelry that evening before going to sleep. And we just wanted to clear that fact up as it is a highly believed scenario in the overall storyline.

I will also suggest that everyone PLEASE read the trial transcripts of Halina Czaban's testimony at Darlie's trial.

Some statements were made in her testimony that claims that she believed that Darlie may have been trying to suffocate baby Drake on that day.

However, I will say that her statement that Darlie may have been trying to suffocate baby Drake was not a topic of major focus by the police or the prosecutor during the trial, my opinion is that we have to question if the police considered her a reliable witness.

And numerous comments were made in her testimony that may make a reader believe that Darlie was not in the right frame of mind before Darin returning home that evening.

Halina Czaban also testified about seeing a black sports car in front of Darlie's house on the 5th of June as she left for the day.

She also testified that she had seen a black sports car in the area two months earlier in April.

However, after reading her testimony there is a good chance that the vehicle or vehicles that she said that she witnessed in the area may have belonged there.

The black car that she saw on June 5th was picking somebody up when she noticed it, and she only testified that the driver drove off at a fast rate of speed after picking up the passenger.

And if we throw out the idea that Darlie tried to suffocate Drake that day, then we can dismiss her entire testimony of the events that day, including the black sports car sighting.

Halina and her daughter Basia were leaving just as Darin and Dana were arriving at the house as Darlie was finishing up dinner.

*** When Darin was asked what they had for dinner he stated:

*We ate chicken noodle soup, and **Darlie had made homemade bread** when Helena was there, and, Helena was going to teach Darlie some new dishes from Poland.*

The boys were playing outside with the neighborhood kids, riding their bikes on the sidewalk, as they were not allowed to ride their bikes in the street.

As Darlie was finishing up dinner, Darin and Dana played with baby Drake.

Darlie stated to the police that Damon came inside from playing with his friends first and Devon called the house shortly after.

Darlie said that she told him to be home soon because we were going to eat.

Devon came home shortly after the phone call and Darlie, Darin and both of the boys, and the baby, and Darlie's sister Dana, all ate dinner together.

*** Darlie's statement to the Rowlett P.D. on June 8, (two days after the murders) she states:

After we ate we cleaned all the plates. I was changing Drake while Darin put everything in some containers for leftovers.

So from the statements of Darin and Darlie, we know that they had homemade bread for dinner and that the dishes were cleaned right after dinner was over.

This may not be a significant statement to some people, and the pro-Darlie groups will not focus on the fact that the family had homemade bread that night with their meal.

And you may be asking what the significance is of this fact?

From these statements, we can come to two very important conclusions.

#1 the bread knife was most likely used to cut the homemade bread that Darlie made for dinner. (One could say that it is almost 100% likely that a person would cut fresh bread with a bread knife and not another type of knife)

#2 the bread knife would have been washed with the rest of the dishes and left out on the countertop to dry with the other dishes from dinner that night.

We know that the dishes were left out to air dry on the countertop by viewing crime scene photos of the kitchen showing the dishes on the counter left out to air dry.

The following photo is an actual still shot from the Rowlett police crime scene video of the inside of the Routier's home.

You can see in the picture that the dishes are located to the left of the kitchen sink left out to air dry.

And in those dishes would have been the bread knife that was used to cut the homemade bread that Darlie cooked for dinner that evening.

In this photo, you can see the dishes on the counter, air drying.

On June 8, (2 days after the murders) Darlie told the Rowlett police that after dinner Darin, Dana, and she talked a little about how happy they were that their business had been busy for the past three weeks and that they hoped it would continue since work had been slow for a couple of months.

Devon and Damon went outside to play with one of their friends while Darin, Dana, and her just sat around and watched a little TV.

During this first interview, there is no mention of any activities after dinner that happened outside of the Routier's kitchen and living room area.

*** *All of the movements of the three adults from the time that dinner ended to Darin taking Dana home are centered only in those two areas of the home.*

When Darin was questioned on June 8, he said nothing about what he did immediately following dinner. He started his statement after he returned home later that evening after taking Dana home.

*** *However, seven months later when Darlie went to trial in the last week of January 1997 additional events of June 6th were added in both of their testimonies.*

Some people who are supporters of Darlie say that they BOTH just forgot to mention these events to the police when questioned. While those who believe that Darlie is guilty, claim that this new information that they both added to their stories only goes to the cover-up of the real facts in this case.

Now if it was something as insignificant as one of the adults went out to the vehicle or maybe went upstairs to get something for the bay, then yes I would say that it was just a very insignificant action that could have been overlooked.

But this new information is more than just an insignificant event that was so small that it would have been easy to overlook.

Here is the information that was added to their story seven months later.

When Darin was asked during the trial what he did after dinner he stated that he went outside because they had a Pomeranian dog that they had bred the day before, and it was pretty hyper.

He said that Darlie had asked him to go out, and fix the gate on the fence, because it was really hard to open and close, and was dragging the sidewalk whenever it was opened.

He said that he went out, and got all of his tools out of the shed, and shaved off a little bit of the bottom of the gate so that it could the latch better

He was asked in the trial if he was successful in getting the gate fixed.

And his answer was "Yes, sir, I got the latch all lined back up, and I got it to where the gate would swing back and forth, without dragging."

He was also asked for clarification, "Okay. It would swing back and forth so that you wouldn't have to push it with your foot?"

Darin's answer was, "Yes, sir."

He then said that after fixing the gate he went back inside, and played on the floor a little bit with the baby.

And the adults just talked and kind of visited a little bit, and then he took Dana home, at about 9:30.

This information is widely ignored by the Darlie supporters.

They want the world to believe that the gate was hard to open and that Darlie would have a difficult time getting through that gate as it made noise and dragged the ground.

However according to Darin that was not the case, and the Darlie supporters are just spreading false information to sell their version of the murders.

The next bit of information that was added to the story by Darin during the trial, is what many people claim adds more credence to Darlie's guilt.

Darin was asked if he worked in the garage at all that day.

And his answer was that had been talking after supper about the fact that they were possibly going to have a garage sale.

He said that they were not sure if they were going to have it before they went to Pennsylvania on the 14th.

His next statement puzzles people as to how this topic was missed in the prior interviews with the police by both Darin and Darlie.

His exact words in the trial were… **_"So, we were out in the garage, and we were kind of -- had been separating it._**

He did not say that "HE" was out in the garage; he said that "WE" were out in the garage.

He was then asked if the garage door up or down while they were in the garage.

He stated that the "garage door was up, **_while we were_** working"

Again, he uses the plural "WE" when talking about working in the garage. However, before this date, neither of them has ever stated this.

I will not focus much on the word "we" versus "I" in Darin's testimony.

However, I will say that when a person is testifying they are recalling facts of the case that they remember as they remember it to have happened.

If the person is saying "WE" then he must remember it as, "him and someone else" in the storyline of his memory. If he is lying about the events he may mistakenly say "WE" when he should have said just "I".

He then goes on to add in the fact that it was really hot out in the garage.

He said that it seemed like it was about 106 or 108 degrees. It was extremely hot.

Unfortunately for Darin, this new statement opened the door for the next question, "Were the windows up or down?"

He said that one of the windows was up, probably six inches -- six to eight inches over by the cat cage.

Now we get to the information about the family's full-blooded Persian attack cat named Bear.

He said that he had built the cage to breed cats and that he had bought Darlie two cats for Christmas.

He said that the cage was probably four foot by probably seven feet tall, and he had built it where it was bi-level so that they could have one cat on the top, and one cat on the bottom.

And when they had their babies, they could secure them down in the bottom.

He said that they even planned to put lamps inside of the cage to keep them warm.

This is a still frame from the police video taken inside of the Routier's garage that shows the huge cat cage next to the window where the Routiers claimed the murderer entered the home.

He then testifies about the cat that they called Bear that he said was, "just really a weird cat."

He also added, "That cat didn't like nobody. I mean, the kids wouldn't come around that cat for nothing. I mean, he would just hiss at you, like he was going to come out of that cage any minute."

So now, thanks to Darin's testimony we learned about the wild cat that "would just hiss at you like he was going to come out of that cage any minute."

Darin was then asked if the cat was kept in the garage.

His answer to this question has been a major topic of debate for the pro and anti-Darlie camps over the years.

Darin's statement was, "*He was kept in the garage, and Darlie ended up going and buying another cage to put inside of the house, because it was cruelty to that cat, to be stuck out there in the garage when it's a hundred degrees, and it was probably 120 degrees on his skin because it was so hot out there.*"

He said that they ended up bringing the cat in. and Darlie went and bought another cat cage, and they had it inside the house, "So that it could get some air conditioning."

He also stated that when he went inside the house, he had left the window open that was open about six inches next to the cat's cage.

Now you may be wondering why we focused on the family's "weird cat" as Darin called it.

We know that the cat cage story of Darin's testimony is 100% true because the police took photos of the Routier's living room right after the murders.

And in one of the photos (state's exhibit 150), you can see the cat cage just feet from where Darlie said that she was sleeping.

Many people believe that if the cat would as Darin said, "just hiss at you like he was going to come out of that cage any minute."

Then why didn't he hiss and act like he was going to come out of his cage that night when Darlie and Devon were being attacked just feet from the cage.

And if the cat did act out like Darin described, then why didn't Darlie wake up to the sounds of the cat making noise?

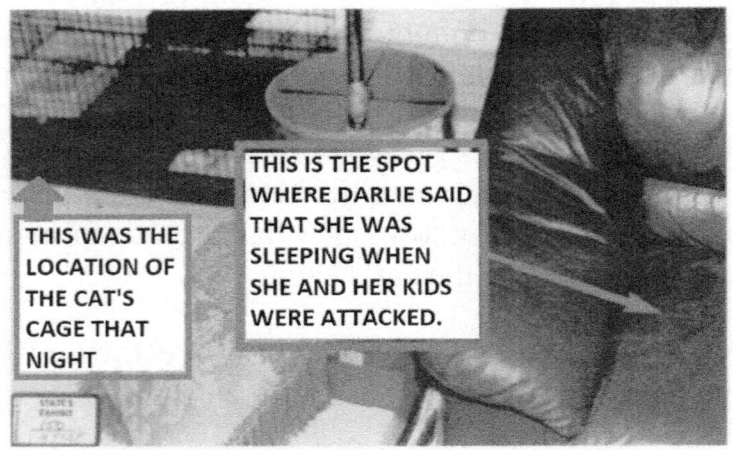

Many pro-Darlie people claim that she was nowhere near the cat's cage that night so she would not have heard the cat.

Here is a hand-drawn sketch that was drawn by Darlie showing where she slept AND what end of the couch her head was at while she slept.

32

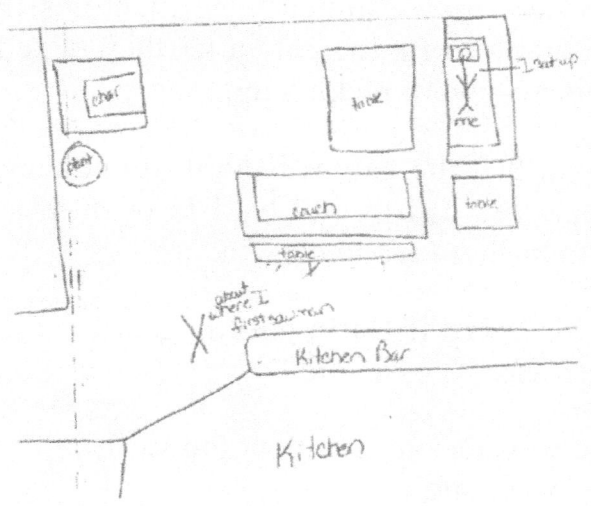

Fig. 1-1 Darlie's diagram of scene when she was awakened

Page 3

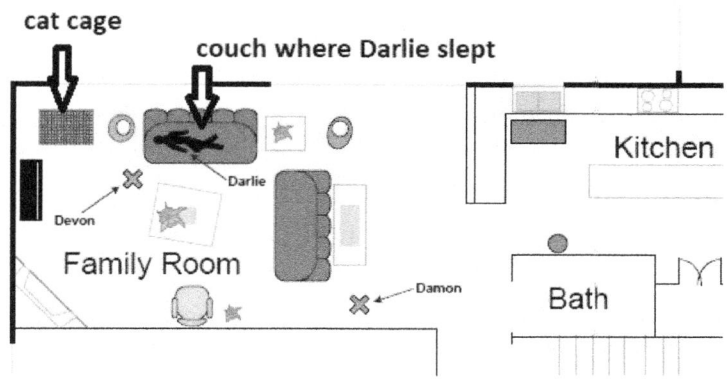

And to clear up any confusion that a reader may have here is a sketch of the crime scene.

33

In Darlie's trial testimony she mentions that she asked Darin to fix the gate after they talked about the business work picking up.

She said that the gate was hard to open and close and that you had to pull hard to open it, and you have to push it hard to close it.

She was asked if Darin got the gate fixed and her answer was, "Yes he did."

Darlie was questioned about the stuff in the garage for the yard sale.

She said that after he fixed the gate he went into the garage to sort through the yard sale stuff. And after he finished he came inside the house.

She did not say that she was in the garage with Darin that evening.

Darlie said that she asked Darin to drive Dana home because she wasn't feeling too well.

There are some questions about where Dana Stahl lived the night of the boy's murders.

The District Attorney said that she lived in Garland at the time of the murders.

However, Darlie's mother Darlie Kee stated that she lived in Plano Texas with her.

When asked, "Where do you live now?"

She answered, "I live in Plano, Texas."

Some people falsely claim that she moved to Plano shortly after the murders.

However, she was then asked, "How long have you lived in Plano?"

And her answer was, "Since 1993."

She also told the court that her daughter Dana Stahl lived with her at the time.

People are focusing on this information to throw doubt into the case about how long Darin should have been gone that evening to take Dana home.

Some say that he was gone far too long while others claim that he wasn't gone long enough.

So let's look at the travel time from Rowlett Plano.

We will also add in five extra minutes to consider the time that Darin would have to stop at any traffic lights and the time he would be at Dana's house dropping her off.

Plano is 21 minutes from 5801 Eagle Dr, Rowlett, Texas.

This would also be about 46 minutes round trip when we add in the 5 extra minutes for stops.

The state attorney's location was Garland, which is only 17 minutes from 5801 Eagle Dr, Rowlett, Texas.

This would be about 39 minutes round trip when we add in the 5 extra minutes for stops.

Even Darin testified, "It's only a 20-minute drive or a 30-minute drive over there."

So no matter where he went that night, either Plano or Garland he would have been gone between 40-50 minutes minimum.

Many people are fixated on the fact that Darlie testified in the trial, "about 20 or 25 minutes later Darin came in and sat down with us while we watched TV."

They say that no matter where Darin went, he could not have been back home in 20 or 25 minutes.

In response to that, I will say that I doubt that Darlie was paying that much attention to the time frame and we should not spend too much energy on the time frame that he was gone as it does not tell us who killed Damon and Devon that night.

She did say that about 8 - 8:30, that she told the boys that they needed to tell their friends that they needed to go home, that it was time to come in.

She thinks that Devon had said something about wanting to spend the night with a friend, but he had just had a little boy named Michael over the night before.

She also said that they had kind of gotten in a little bit of trouble from their father, for emptying all of the water of the hot tub.

Darlie told Damon and Devon that they needed to go upstairs and get dry clothes on.

When they went upstairs, Darlie vacuumed the rug by the sliding glass doors because according to her statement, they had drug in quite a bit of dirt off of their feet.

Darlie was asked in the trial where she had left the vacuum after she used it and her answer was, by the bar.

And this is where the police found it tipped over at.

Many of the Anti-Darlie people say that Darlie never used the vacuum that evening to clean up after the boys came inside.

But in this sketch, you can see the location where Halina stated that she left the vacuum and where Darlie stated that she left the vacuum.

This clearly shows that the vacuum was moved from the location where Halina put it and where the police found it.

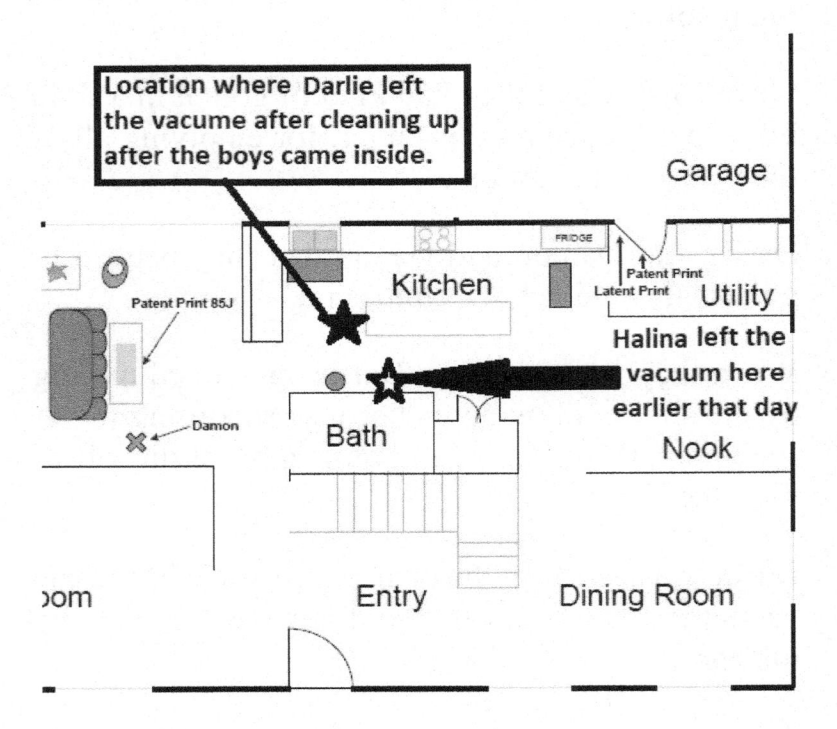

While Darin was gone taking Dana home, the boys brought down their blankets and pillows and asked if they could watch TV.

Darlie said that it was okay, and they came downstairs and played on the floor in front of the TV with Drake while she made popcorn.

At Darlie's bail hearing Darin testified just one month after the murders, that he drove Dana home at 9:00 and returned home around 9:40.

However, at Darlie's trial, he states that he returned home at around 10:15.

This change may have been made to better fit the scenario that Darlie put forth in her defense. Or it could just be a mistake in his version of the events.

Many people have focused a lot of attention on this time frame. If we consider that the trip to take Dana home was at max, 30 minutes one way then the time frame fits for the one-hour roundtrip.

We will just stick with the fact that he did take Dana home that evening.

For about two weeks before that evening, Dana was staying at the Routier's home. (This was discovered in Darin's trial testimony)

However, for some unknown reason, Darlie told Darin to take her home that evening.

The only red flag that comes to mind for me is that Dana was working at Testnec Electronics with Darin at the time.

So, if he drove Dana home that night, then he would have to make the 1-hour round trip again in the morning to pick her up to go to work with him.

He also testified at trial that Darlie was watching TV as she lay on the couch, and Devon was already asleep on the floor in front of the big screen TV.

And Damon was still awake lying on his blanket curled up a little black kitty that the family had.

He said that the baby was lying on Darlie's chest.

They watched TV in the living room until Drake woke up and started to get fussy.

Darlie said that she got up and made him a bottle.

Darin told the police in his first interviews that Drake had fallen asleep about 10-10:30, and that he took him up to bed in his and Darlie's bedroom.

He said that he put a blanket on him and turned out lights.

At Darlie's trial, he testified that he went and got a bottle, and then took him from Darlie, and went upstairs and watched the news for a little while.

He testified that he held him in the rocking chair, and watched the news for a little while in the TV room.

He said that it took Probably 30 minutes or so for drake to fall asleep.

After drake fell asleep, Darin placed him in his crib and put his blankets on him, and then went back downstairs.

Just After Midnight

When Darin came back downstairs he and Darlie talked about a few problems they were having with the car and the boat.

Darlie said that since she had the baby she was having some depression. She also told Darin that she was depressed because she hadn't been able to take the boys anywhere. After all, they only had one car seeing that Darin's Jaguar was broke down and he was driving her Pathfinder.

In both of their initial interviews with the police, they both downplay the conversation that they had that night.

They tell the police about how they discussed the vacation that Darlie was going to go on even though they were basically out of money and could not afford a vacation seeing that they were planning a trip to Pennsylvania the very next week.

Darin mentions that they spoke about the fact that the boys were not being able to start baseball yet because they were so busy with the baby.

He said that they talked about the business and their bills.

In Darin's statement to the police, he stated that "Darlie was having a hard time with taking care of the baby (all) today."

Some people have pointed out that the boys were not able to start baseball yet *"because they were so busy with the baby."*

And that Darlie told Darin that, *"Darlie was having a hard time with taking care of the baby (all) today."*

Some have said over the years that it seemed as though Darlie was getting overwhelmed with taking care of Drake.

One very important fact that both Darlie and Darin left out in their early statements was that they were having a little more than just a "discussion" regarding issues in their lives.

In July 2002, Darin made a sworn statement where he states that on the evening of June 5, 1996, he had a verbal disagreement with Darlie and that during that discussion, she asked him for a martial separation.

However, Darlie doesn't paint this picture in her statement to the police.

She said that Darin told her that he loved her and asked if she wanted him to sleep downstairs with her because she wanted to stay up a little and watch TV.

She said that she told him no because she didn't think he would be able to sleep on the couch with her and get any sleep.

This next statement that she made is a very important topic for the anti-Darlie camp.

Darlie told the police that she had been sleeping on the couch for the past week or so off and on because the baby slept in their room in the crib and whenever he moved he woke her up.

At the time Drake was just eight months old and you wouldn't think that a baby that young could cause enough noise just by moving in a crib to wake Darlie up. But in her statement, she says that it would.

Many of the anti-Darlie people will say that if a baby moving around in a crib will wake you up, then why didn't your two sons being brutally murdered just feet from where you slept never woke you?

Darin said that he went upstairs to get Darlie a blanket and pillow and came back downstairs to cover her up.

He said that they talked a little more about her going to Cancun with some friends across the street.

Darlie said that Darin and she laid together for a little while on the couch until around 12:30 or 1:00.

Darin then decided to go upstairs to bed because he had work the next day.

Darin said that he told Darlie to dream about him and went upstairs around 1:00 am.

She said that Darin kissed her goodnight and said he loved her, and she told him that she loved him and would see him in the morning.

Darin told the police that when he went to bed that the boys were asleep with pillows and blankets on the floor.

EVERYONE'S LOCATION WHEN DARIN WENT TO BED AROUND 1:00

Devon was asleep face up in front of the TV and Damon was asleep between the couch and coffee table next to where Darlie was sleeping.

When Darin got to his bedroom he checked on Drake.

He said that he couldn't get to sleep so he watched TV for 10 to 15 min.

When he started to get sleepy he took his glasses off and turned the TV off.

He said that he could not go to sleep for a while but finally he fell asleep.

Darlie said that she eventually fell asleep.

We will note that in the morning when the police arrived the television was still on.

This will be a subject of topic later in the story.

Before we finish this chapter I would like to return to the statement that Darin made in 2002 regarding the fact that Darlie asked for a separation.

In that same statement he also stated that in 1994, he arranged for his Jaguar to be stolen.

It was from this statement that we also learned that in March or April 1996, he had asked his father-in-law Robbie Gene Kee, if he knew anyone who would agree to burglarize his home as part of an insurance scam.

He said that he would arrange for everyone to be gone from the house and that someone who he would hire would come to the house and take away the furniture and other items from the house using a U-Haul truck.

He also stated that he would then pay that person from the proceeds of the resulting insurance payments.

He also added that between March and May 1996, he had told multiple people of the planned insurance scam.

If we take a moment and look at this statement about the insurance scam we can see a major issue right off the bat.

Right from the start, the Routiers were trying to come up with a plausible reason as to why someone would want to come into their home in the middle of the night.

After the initial investigation, the police ruled out burglary as the valuables that were left on the counter in plain sight were never taken.

However, the Routiers and Darlie's family had to create a plausible explanation as to why someone entered the house that night.

And I truly believe that is why Darin came forward with the story about the insurance scam and the fact that he "had told multiple people of the planned insurance scam."

I truly believe that the story about the insurance scam was made up to create reasonable doubt in the mind of the public to sway their opinion about Darlie's guilt.

Many people don't agree with me on this and use the "insurance scam plot" as a reason to have Darlie killed off.

My only response to that is this…

If the insurance scam was real and Darin had mentioned this to multiple people, then why did it take him five years to say anything about it?

If my wife was facing the death penalty for killing my kids and our only defense is that someone broke into our home and committed the crime then I would have shared this very important bit of information very early in the investigation.

But let's take this one more step further...

Let's say that Darin did forget that he had tried to set up the very same scenario that played out in his home that night (except for maybe the killings of his two boys) and never told a word of this to the police.

What are the chances that his father-in-law forgot the insurance scam plot too?

Darlie's stepfather, Robbie Gene Kee, never told anyone about this insurance scam plot either.

Now you would think that if your step-daughter was facing the death penalty and you had known that her husband had approached you to carry out a burglary that this would be something that you would mention to the police.

Or at the very least to your wife…

NOPE! Just like Darin, he forgot about the insurance scam plot or else didn't think that it was significant information to share with anyone.

About three years after Darlie is convicted and sentenced to death, Robbie Gene Keen all of a sudden remembers the insurance scam and tells his wife who relays the information to Darlie's attorney Stephen Cooper.

Another interesting fact came up in this statement that I feel needs to be addressed here.

I feel that all of the information regarding this statement needs to be addressed here not just the part that points out the possible guilt of Darlie.

In this statement, he said that he first met with attorney Douglas Mulder in July 1996.

He said that he met at least once a week with Mulder in July 1996.

He said that the reason for the meetings was Mr. Mulder's potential representation of Darlie and him in her criminal trial.

I want to point out that he stated that Mulder was going to potentially represent "BOTH Darlie and him" in her criminal trial.

He said that Mulder told him in august 1996, that Darlie's court-appointed attorneys, Wayne Huff and Douglas Parks, had confided in him that they were going to try and portray Darin as the person who murdered Damon and Devon because they thought that he had something to do with the deaths of his sons.

Now we can see how a defense attorney, in his course of defending his client, would try to point at someone else rather than his client.

And that could be the reasoning behind the fact that they were trying to paint Darin as the murderer.

But let's stop right here for a moment!

At this time, his wife is being accused of murdering his two boys. And he now learns that he is being looked at as a possible killer instead of his wife, and he still fails to mention that he had tried to set up an insurance scam.

He can't even remember that he set up the insurance scam to defend himself! This makes me wonder if the insurance scam story wasn't concocted later just to build support for Darlie after she was convicted.

He also stated that he told Mulder that if he was hired, that Darin did not want him to "go after" him.

Mr. Mulder agreed that, if he was hired to represent Darlie, he would not argue as part of the defense that Darin was in any way a suspect.

So, instead of telling Mulder about the insurance scam and giving crucial information that could point to someone besides his wife, he chooses to make sure that he is not implicated in the murders!

On October 21, 1996, Mr. Mulder became lead counsel in Darlie's criminal trial.

Darin Waking Up Until The 911 Call

We are going to look at Darlie and Darin's statements to the Rowlett P.D., on June 8, 1996, statements made during Darlie's court hearing on September 12, 1996, and their trial testimony on January 28, 1997.

We will also note that the human brain retains the most memory of an event within the first few days of the event.

It is a proven fact that the most memorable parts of the event are retained in the hours and days right after the vent. And that is why most police investigators are adamant about getting a victim's statement as soon as possible after the event.

You can look up the "Ebbinghaus Forgetting Curve" to research more on the brain's rate of forgetting information.

Ebbinghaus Forgetting Curve

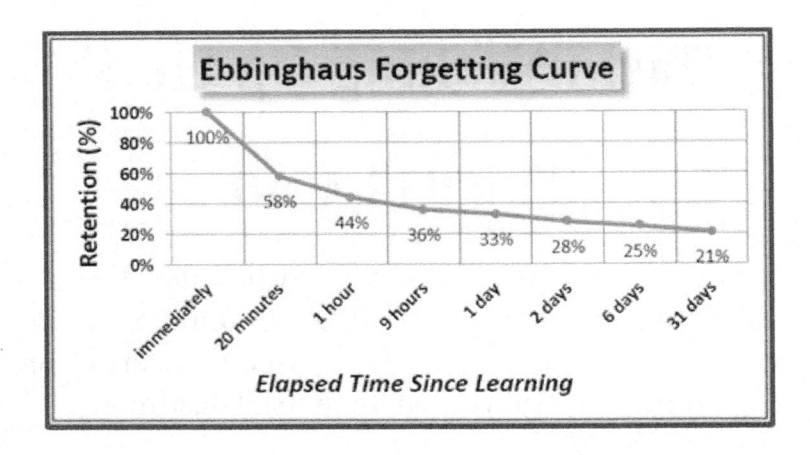

Elapsed Time	Retention
immediately	100%
20 minutes	58%
1 hour	44%
9 hours	36%
1 day	33%
2 days	28%
6 days	25%
31 days	21%

So we will place a lot of focus on Darin and Darlie's first statements to the police after the murders to recreate the events of June 6, 1996.

And we will add in their trial testimony to compare their first statements against their trial testimony.

I will put their trial testimony in *<u>italics and underlined it</u>* to separate it from their first statement that they made to the police following the murders.

I will note that the trial testimony was made on January 28 & 29, 1997. (Seven months after the murders occurred)

This would have given both Darin and Darlie time to sort out the events of that night in preparation for trial.

In her statement on June 8, 1996, Darlie said that she was asleep but woke when she felt Damon press on her right shoulder and heard him cry.

She said that this really made her come awake.

She said that she then realized that a man was standing down at her feet walking away from her.

She told the police that she walked after him and that is when she heard glass breaking.

She got halfway through the kitchen and decided to turn back around to run and turn on the light.

QUESTION: *All right, Darlie, what is the very next thing that you remember, that you either felt or heard or saw?*

DARLIE'S ANSWER: *the next thing that I remember is Damon hitting my right shoulder, and he said "Mommy," or he said "Mommy, Mommy," I'm not sure, but he said, "Mommy." I looked up, and you've got to remember that I'm in a -- I am not completely awake, you know, when you first wake up; you are not completely wide awake. And there was a man that was down, going away from the couches, walking away from me. I started to get up and when I stood up, I heard noise like glass breaking. I started to walk towards the kitchen, Damon was behind me, and when I got to the kitchen, I put my hand back here for Damon to stay. And when I got to the kitchen, I could see the guy going into the utility room.*

NOTE: In both statements, she does not state that she woke to the man on top of her and her fighting him off.

She said that she then ran back towards the utility room and that is when she realized that there was a big white-handled knife lying on the floor.

She said that it was then that she first realized that she had blood all over herself.

She said that she grabbed the knife thinking that the man was in the garage and might still be there.

It was at this time that she yelled for Darin.

She said that she ran back through the kitchen and that is when she realized that the entire living area had blood all over everything.

She then put the knife on the counter and ran into the entrance, turned on a light, and started screaming again for Darin.

QUESTION: *Were the lights on?*

DARLIE'S ANSWER: *No, sir, the lights were off.*

QUESTION: *Okay. So the area was illuminated by the big screen TV set only?*

DARLIE'S ANSWER: *There was a little bit of -- yeah, I mean, there was a little bit of light, I don't know what you would call that, just kind of a --*

QUESTION: *Okay.*

DARLIE'S ANSWER: *A glare, maybe.*

NOTE: Darlie testified that the big screen TV was on that night and the responding officer said that the TV was on when he arrived at the house.

These are pictures of the garage window with the cut screen and the living room window.

I placed a star in both pictures located at the same spot in the backyard to give you a reference point.

One thing that many of the Darlie supporters claim is that the killer did not know that anyone was home that night.

If anyone came into that backyard at night, in the dark, they would have noticed the glare of the TV that was on in the living room as the blinds were not fully down.

QUESTION: *All right. Okay. What happened?*

DARLIE'S ANSWER: *I started to take a couple of steps into the kitchen, and I realized that the lights were off, so I turned back around, and I flipped the lights on real quick. I started to walk into the kitchen.*

QUESTION: *Where was the man by this time?*

DARLIE'S ANSWER: *He was gone, he was out of my sight.*

QUESTION: *All right.*

DARLIE'S ANSWER: *I got into the kitchen, and I got to where the island is, there is an island in the middle of the kitchen. I got to where the island was, and it was at that moment that I realized that I had blood on me. And I kept going, walking a little bit, and I saw a knife laying in the utility room. The knife wasn't completely the whole way in the utility room, it was just like, a little bit into the doorway of the utility room. It was an instinct -- I picked up the knife, it was an instinct to pick up the knife. I didn't think about it. It was just an instinct. I picked up the knife, I brought the knife back to the kitchen counter, and set it up on the kitchen counter. At that time, I started to walk into the living room and it was at that time that I saw Devon, and he was laying on the floor, and he wasn't moving and his eyes were open, and he had cuts on him that were so big.*

NOTE: At this point in Darlie's story Darin has not come downstairs yet.

QUESTION: *Did you say anything at that time?*

59

DARLIE'S ANSWER: *I screamed "Devon." I screamed out and I couldn't believe what I was seeing. It was at that time that I turned back around and I went to Damon, and Damon was standing up still.*

QUESTION: *Could you see that he had been hurt or cut or anything at that point?*

DARLIE'S ANSWER: *Not at that time, I couldn't see that he had been hurt. I just started checking all over him and when I turned him around I could see big, huge wounds through his shirt. I started screaming, and I ran into the entranceway, and I flipped on the lights real quick, and I was screaming...*

NOTE: She says that *"I went to Damon, and Damon was standing up still."*

And then she says that she turned him around and that was when she noticed the huge wounds through his shirt.

At this time let's assume that Darin is on his way down the stairs. According to Darlie's testimony, Damon is still fully awake and conscious. And according to Darlie, he was able to stand on his own and according to her, he can understand her and even talk to her.

She thinks that she screamed twice and he ran out of the bedroom with his jeans on and no glasses and was yelling, "what is it, what is it?"

NOTE: In Darlie's first statement to the police she pointed out that Darin "ran out of the bedroom with his jeans on and no glasses". This is an odd statement to make when you are asked to describe what happened at the time of your children's murders. Why did she feel that it was important to point out that Darin was wearing his jeans but not wearing his glasses? And she must have been (or at least felt) that she was 100% sure of these facts to mention them in her first official interview with the police just two days after the murders.

Now I am also going to question why Darin felt that it was necessary to put on his jeans before going down the stairs when he heard his wife screaming and glass breaking?

You would think that if a husband heard a scream from his wife in the middle of the night he would get to her as soon as physically possible.

And why would he take the time to put on the jeans and underwear?

As a parent, I can understand putting on your underwear as you may feel uncomfortable running around naked in front of your kids.

But then again maybe the underwear was still inside of the pants and it was faster to just slide them on and head down the stairs.

She says that she remembers saying he cut them, he tried to kill me, my neck.

Darin ran down the stairs and into the room where the boys were.

DARLIE'S ANSWER: *Darin, Devon, Darin, and Devon, and, we ran back into hallway, Darin went over to Devon, I went into the kitchen and flipped the lights on, and I grabbed the phone, and I went to the drawer where there's towels in the drawer, and I went to the drawer, and I went over to the sink and I got the towels wet.*

NOTE: In her trial testimony was the first time she or Darin states that she went to the sink to get towels. However, they never mention this fact in their first statements to the police.

QUESTION: *You went over to the kitchen, you got the phone, and then what did do you?*

DARLIE'S ANSWER: *I went to the kitchen, and I got the phone, and then I went to the drawer and I got the towels and then I went to the sink.*

QUESTION: *Okay. Why did you get the towels?*

DARLIE'S ANSWER: *I just wanted to help to stop the bleeding. I didn't know what to do. I didn't know what to do. I was just reacting.*

QUESTION: *Okay. So you got the towels?*

DARLIE'S ANSWER: *I got the towels and I went to the sink and I got the towels wet.*

QUESTION: *All right. Were you on the phone with 911?*

DARLIE'S ANSWER: *At that time -- at that time, I think 911 came on.*

It was at this time that she said that she grabbed the phone and called 911.

This is Darin's version of events from waking up and what happened up to the 911 call

In Darin's statement on June 8, 1996, he said that he heard a noise and then Darlie screaming loud.

At trial, he stated that the noise he heard was the glass breaking.

QUESTION: When is the next thing that you heard something of an unusual nature, Darin?

Darin's Answer: The very first thing I hear is the glass break. And then, I hear Darlie screaming, I mean screaming so loud you wouldn't believe it.

Note: In Darlie's statement she heard the glass break as the intruder was running through the kitchen towards the garage door.

Her statement was, "I started to get up and when I stood up, I heard noise like glass breaking."

And before screaming for Darin she stated that she:

1. I started to walk towards the kitchen, Damon was behind me, and when I got to the kitchen, I put my hand back here for Damon to stay.

2. And when I got to the kitchen, I could see the guy going into the utility room.

3. She said that she then ran back towards the utility room and that is when she realized that there was a big white-handled knife lying on the floor.

4. She said that she grabbed the knife thinking that the man was in the garage and might still be there.

5. She brought the knife back to the kitchen counter, and set it up on the kitchen counter.

6. She started to walk into the living room and it was at that time that she saw Devon, and he was laying on the floor, and he wasn't moving and his eyes were open, and he had cuts on him that were so big.

<u>It was at this time that she yelled for Darin.</u>

Maybe there was a longer timeframe between the glass breaking and Darlie yelling that Darin did not elaborate on during questioning at the trial.

However, I want to point out that Darin was on the second floor of the home.

The bedroom where Darin was sleeping on the second floor was not very close to the living room where Darlie and the boys were sleeping.

However, many of Darlie's supporters claim that she fought the intruder off and that it was a very violent interaction. Yet, Darin is woken up by the sound of a wineglass falling off of the wine rack and breaking, but not the sound of Darlie violently fighting off her attacker as her supporters claim happened.

Darin said that Darlie was yelling, "Devon, Devon, Oh my God Devon!"

He told the police that he woke up quickly and grabbed his glasses on the nightstand and ran downstairs as fast as he could.

NOTE: In Darlie's first statement to the police she pointed out that Darin "ran out of the bedroom with his jeans on and no glasses".

At the trial, Darin said that he had both his jeans and his glasses on.

I only focused on Darin's glasses at this point because I wanted to point out the fact that Darlie was so meticulous in her first statement to the police to point out this small detail about Darin's jeans and glasses, yet she leaves out major details in her story about bringing wet towels to her dying sons that she only adds in many months later during her trial.

Darin said that Darlie was at the bottom of the stairs, and while he was running down the stairs, he was thinking that the coffee table had tipped over, and fallen on Devon, because Darlie was screaming, "Devon, Devon, Devon."

He quickly ran into the living room (they called it the Roman room) and ran over to Devon lying on the floor.

He said that he was in the same spot where he was when he saw him last (when he went to bed about 1:00) and knelt over him to see if he was hurt.

He said that he looked at the coffee table to see it tipped over on him. When he looked again at his chest there were two holes in his chest with blood and muscle piercing out.

Because he first thought that the table had fallen on him his first instinct was to look for the broken glass that had cut him.

He said that there wasn't very much blood. And both Darlie and he were screaming, and that they were just freaking out.

NOTE: Many people (both for and against Darlie) have pointed out that in the crime scene photos the coffee table is not in the same position as Darin describes in his testimony.

The table glass top is back on the base and the flowers are back on top of the table.

They are making this tabletop which Darin said was tipped over when he gets downstairs but upright in police photos as some reason to claim that Darlie is innocent.

Darlie's blood was found on top of the glass tabletop in a pattern that indicates that she was standing over top of the table as she was bleeding. And that the glass was in fact on its base.

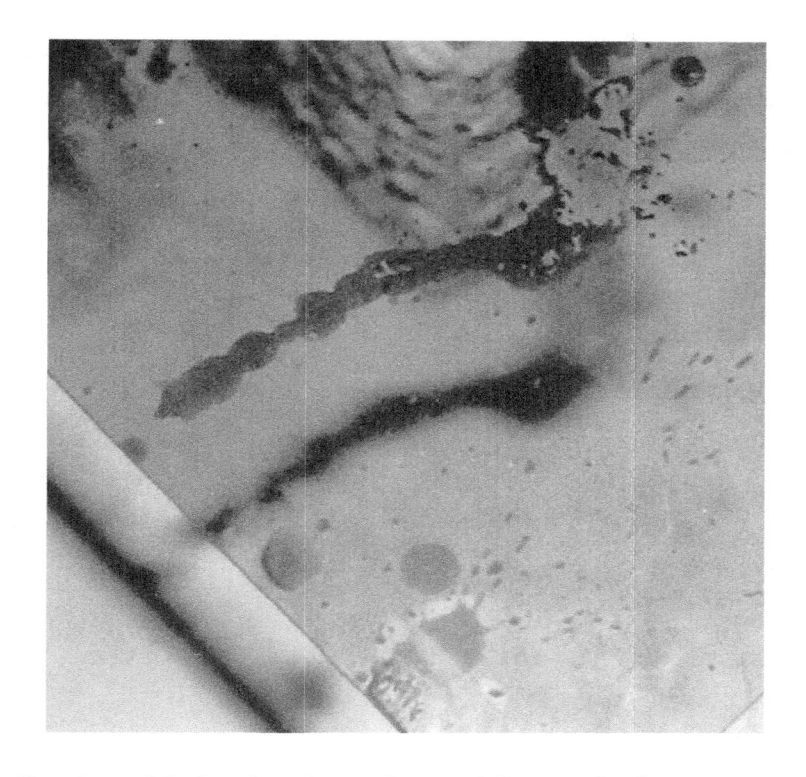

Darin said that he then slapped Devon's face to get him to say something or to look at him.

There was no response, so he started CPR but when he blew into his mouth air came out of his chest.

He said that he blew 5 or 6 times and held his hand over the holes on his chest.

Then when that didn't work he decided to blow into one of the holes in his chest.

In Darin's first statement to the police on June 8th, he pretty much ends the story of events at this point without mentioning anything about Darlie bringing him wet towels.

At this time he looked over at Darlie and she was on the phone calling 911.

The 2:31 a.m. 911 Call

We used the 911 call transcript that is posted on the For Darlie Routier website run by her mother.

This transcript was created from the official tape logs maintained by the Communications Section of the Rowlett Police Department Transcribed by Barry Dickey and Dennis Lowe for Graffiti Productions, Inc.

Darlie's call to 911 started at 2:31 a.m. and lasted five minutes and forty-four seconds.

Here is the 911 call transcript. I will break it down into one-minute sections so that we can review the call in portions. I will point out issues that I see in the 911 call.

00:00:00 911 Operator #1 ...Rowlett 911...what is your emergency...
00:01:19 Darlie Routier ...somebody came here...they broke in...
00:03:27 911 Operator #1 ...ma'am...
00:05:11 Darlie Routier ...they just stabbed me and my children...
00:07:16 911 Operator #1 ...what...
00:08:05 Darlie Routier ...they just stabbed me and my kids...my little boys...

At the start of the call, Darlie states that "THEY" broke in and this would mean multiple people. I will not focus much on that point as we do not know what we would or would not say in the same situation.

00:09:24 911 Operator #1 ...who...who did...
00:11:12 Darlie Routier ...my little boy is dying...

Before this statement, she was focusing on both boys when talking to the 911 dispatcher. Yet she is now only saying that only one of her little boys is dying.

00:11:25 RADIO ...(unintelligible) clear...
00:13:07 911 Operator #1 ...hang on ...hang on... hang on
00:15:03 Darlie Routier ...hurry... (unintelligible)...
00:16:01 911 Operator #1 ...stand by for medical emergency
00:18:11 Darlie Routier ...ma'am...
00:18:19 911 Operator #1 ...hang on ma'am...
00:21:26 Darlie Routier ...ma'am...
00:23:00 911 Operator #1 ...unknown medical emergency... 5801 Eagle Drive...
00:24:00 RADIO ...(unintelligible)...
00:26:24 Darlie Routier ...ma'am...
00:27:12 911 Operator #1 ...ma'am... I'm trying to get an ambulance to you... hang on a minute...
00:28:20 RADIO ... (siren)...

00:29:13 Darlie Routier ...oh my God ...my babies are dying...

At this point, she is back to referencing both boys.

00:30:12 Darin Routier ...(unintelligible)...
00:31:09 911 Operator #1 ...what's going on ma'am...
00:32:13 Darlie Routier ...(unintelligible) ...oh my God...
00:33:49 RADIO ...(tone - signal broadcast)...
00:34:01 Background Voice ...(unintelligible)...
00:35:20 Darlie Routier ...(unintelligible) thought he was dead ...oh my God...
00:39:08 Darin Routier ...(unintelligible)...
00:39:29 Darlie Routier ...I don't even know (unintelligible)...

We need to look at the interaction between Darin and Darlie at the 39-second point in the call. Darin asked Darlie a question to which her answer was, "I don't even know". We can only imagine what he asked her. We could only assume the question was, "who did this?" or something similar.

00:40:22 911 Operator #1 ...attention 901 unknown medical emergency 5801...
00:42:23 Darin Routier ...(unintelligible)...
00:43:15 Darlie Routier ...I don't even know (unintelligible)...

At this point, it seems as though Darin may have asked Darlie the same question a second time.

In the audio transcript, it sounds like she is answering, "I don't even know who did it Darin."

00:44:04 911 Operator #1 ...Eagle Drive ...Box 238 ...cross street Linda Vista and Willowbrook ...attention 901 medical emergency...
00:49:28 Darlie Routier ...who was breathing...
00:40:10 Darin Routier ...(unintelligible)...
00:51:15 Darlie Routier ...(unintelligible) are they still laying there (unintelligible)...
00:51:19 911 Operator #1 ...may be possible stabbing ...5801 Eagle Drive ...Box 238 ...cross street Linda Vista and Willowbrook...
00:55:06 Darlie Routier ...oh my God ...what do we do...
00:57:17 911 Operator #1 ...time out 2:32...
00:58:26 Darlie Routier ...oh my God...
00:58:28 911 Operator #1 ...stamp me a card Clint...

In the first minute of the 911 call, we see what would be expected of a mother who is faced with the stabbing of her two boys. Darlie is stressing for help to hurry up and get to the house.

01:01:02 911 Operator #1 ...80...
01:01:16 RADIO ...(unintelligible)...
01:02:13 Darlie Routier ...oh my God...

01:03:05 RADIO ...(unintelligible)...
01:04:07 911 Operator #1 ...need units going towards 5801 Eagle Drive ...5801 Eagle Drive
01:04:07 Darlie Routier ...oh my God ...my baby's dead...

This is a very odd statement for a mother to make. In most instances, a mother is the last person to accept that their child has died. When told that a child has died most mothers would automatically deny the facts and say things like, "No you're wrong, my child's alive." or make statements like, "NO! My baby is still alive!"

Very rarely does a mother immediately claim that their child is dead. Especially when just seconds earlier, she was begging for help to arrive to save them from dying.

01:07:08 Darlie Routier ...Damon ...hold on honey...
01:08:11 Darin Routier ...(unintelligible)...
01:08:22 911 Operator #1 ...hysterical female on the phone...
01:10:03 Darlie Routier ...(unintelligible)...
01:10:10 Darin Routier ...(unintelligible)...
01:10:26 911 Operator #1 ...says her child has been stabbed
01:11:28 Darlie Routier ...I saw them Darin...

This time she once again says "them" when talking about the killer. This use of the word "them" would be odd as she has already been on the call for over a minute and she is now replying to a comment that Darin had made to her and not franticly calling for help to a 911 operator.

01:12:21 Darin Routier ...oh my God ...(unintelligible) ...came in here...
01:14:10 911 Operator #1 ...ma'am ...I need you to calm down and talk to me...
01:14:24 RADIO ...(unintelligible)...
01:16:25 Darlie Routier ...ok...
01:16:26 SOUND ...(unintelligible)...
01:17:12 911 Operator #1 ...twice Clint...
01:18:26 Darlie Routier ...didn't you get my address...
01:20:19 911 Operator #1 ...5801 Eagle...
01:22:00 Darlie Routier ...yes ...we need help...
01:22:03 RADIO ...(unintelligible) will be enroute code...
01:24:20 Darlie Routier ...Darin ...I don't know who it was...

Why would Darlie feel the need to tell Darin that she didn't know who stabbed her boys? And why would she be asked that by Darin?

01:24:23 911 Operator #1 ...2:33 code...
01:26:15 Darlie Routier ...we got to find out who it was...

01:27:12 911 Operator #1 ...ma'am...
01:28:04 911 Operator #1 ...ma'am listen ...listen to me...
01:29:27 Darlie Routier ...yes ...yes ...(unintelligible)...
01:30:23 RADIO ...(unintelligible) I'm clear ...do you need anything...
01:32:08 Darin Routier ...(unintelligible)...
01:32:20 Darlie Routier ...oh my God...
01:34:00 911 Operator #1 ...(unintelligible)...
01:34:22 911 Operator #1 ...do you take the radio Clint...
01:35:23 911 Operator #2 ...yes...
01:36:12 Darlie Routier ...oh my God...
01:36:25 911 Operator #1 ...I...ma'am...
01:38:03 Darlie Routier ...yes...
01:38:17 911 Operator #1 ...I need you to ...
01:38:23 RADIO ...(unintelligible) start that way (unintelligible)... will revise...
01:39:28 911 Operator #1 ...I need you to talk to me...
01:41:21 Darlie Routier ...what ...what ...what...
01:44:25 RADIO ...(unintelligible)...
01:44:28 Darlie Routier ...my babies are dead (unintelligible)...

Darlie states again that her boys are dead.

01:46:20 RADIO ...go ahead and start that way ...siren code 4 ...advise...
01:47:10 Darlie Routier ...(unintelligible)...

77

01:48:03 Darlie Routier ...(unintelligible) do you want honey ...hold on (unintelligible)...
01:49:17 911 Operator #1 ...ma'am ...I can't understand you...
01:50:21 Darlie Routier ...yes...
01:51:18 911 Operator #1 ...you're going to have to slow down ...calm down ...and talk to me...
01:52:19 Darlie Routier ...I'm talking to my babies ...they're dying...

Darlie now goes back to the statement that the boys are dying and not dead.
01:55:03 911 Operator #1 ...what is going on...
01:56:29 Darlie Routier ...somebody came in while I was sleeping ...me and my little boys were sleeping downstairs...
This is a strange answer to the 911 operator's question, "What is going on?"

On many different occasions throughout the call, she adds information that is not reverent to the call. A mother would be more focused on the time that it is taking for the paramedics to arrive or the police to come and catch the intruder.

It is as though she is making a statement regarding the activities that she wants the police to know.

02:02:00 RADIO ... (unintelligible) I'll be clear...
02:02:20 Darlie Routier ...some man ...came in ...stabbed my babies ...stabbed me ...I woke up ...I

was fighting ...he ran out through the garage ...threw the knife down ...my babies are dying ...they're dead ...oh my God...

This one statement caused a major red flag in her story of events.

some man ...came in ...

Stabbed my babies ... <u>Boys stabbed first</u>

Stabbed me ... <u>She was asleep and slept through her boy's brutal attacks.</u>

I woke up ...<u> and even slept through her attack.</u>

I was fighting ... <u>Darlie later stated in trial that she said that she was "frightened" and not "fighting" at this point in the call.</u>

He ran out through the garage ... <u>This part of the statement makes sense in a call for help to tell the 911 dispatcher which way the killer left the house.</u>

Threw the knife down ...<u>Why would she tell the 911 dispatcher this information? It has no significance to the reasoning behind the 911 call, which is to call for help and get the help to your house as soon as possible.</u>

My babies are dying ... <u>She first says that the boys are dying.</u>

They're dead ... <u>However; in the very next breath they are dead.</u>

02:14:23 911 Operator #1 ...ok ...stay on the phone with me...
02:16:11 Darin Routier ...(unintelligible)...
02:17:06 Darlie Routier ...oh my God...
02:17:29 911 Operator #1 ...what happened (unintelligible) dispatch 901...
02:20:15 Darlie Routier ...hold on honey ...hold on...
02:22:01 911 Operator #1 ...(unintelligible) who was on (unintelligible)...
02:22:26 911 Operator #2 ...it was (unintelligible) the white phone...
02:23:08 Darlie Routier ...hold on...
02:25:26 911 Operator #2 ...they were wondering when we need to dispatch ...so I sent a double team...
02:25:28 Darlie Routier ...oh my God ...oh my God...
02:28:08 911 Operator #1 ...ok ...thanks...
02:28:21 Darlie Routier ...oh my God...
02:29:20 SOUND ...(unintelligible)...
02:30:01 Darlie Routier ...oh my God...
02:30:20 911 Operator #1 ...ma'am...
02:31:06 RADIO ...(unintelligible)...
02:31:14 911 Operator #1 ...who's there with you...
02:32:15 Darlie Routier ...Karen ...(unintelligible)...

80

Karen was a neighbor who lived across the street who worked in the hospital. It seems as though Darlie went to the door and yelled out to Karen in hope that she would come to assist them.

02:33:15 911 Operator #1 ...ma'am...
02:34:06 Darlie Routier ...what...
02:38:11 911 Operator #1 ...is there anybody in the house ...besides you and your children...
02:38:11 Darlie Routier ...no ...my husband he just ran downstairs ...he's helping me ...but they're dying ...oh my God ...they're dead...

Again they went from dying to dead in a matter of seconds.

02:43:24 911 Operator #1 ...ok ...ok ...how many little boys ...is it two boys...
02:46:06 Darin Routier ...(unintelligible)...
02:46:25 Darlie Routier ...there's two of 'em ...there's two...
02:48:18 RADIO ...what's the cross street on that address on Eagle...
02:50:15 Darlie Routier ...oh my God ...who would do this...
02:53:13 911 Operator #1 ...(unintelligible) listen to me ...calm down ...(unintelligible)...
02:53:21 Darlie Routier ...I feel really bad ...I think I'm dying...
02:55:06 RADIO ...228...
02:56:06 911 Operator #1 ...go ahead...

02:58:12 RADIO ...(unintelligible) address again (unintelligible)...

02:59:12 RADIO ...(unintelligible)...

02:59:22 Darlie Routier ...when are they going to be here...

03:00:22 911 Operator #1 ...5801 Eagle Drive ...5801 Eagle Drive...

03:03:28 Darlie Routier ...when are they going to be here...

03:03:29 911 Operator #1 ...going to be a stabbing...

03:05:20 Darlie Routier ...when are they going to be here...

03:06:20 911 Operator #1 ...ma'am ...they're on their way...

03:08:00 RADIO ...(unintelligible)...

03:08:08 Darlie Routier ...I gotta just sit here forever ...oh my God...

03:11:14 911 Operator #1 ...2:35...

03:12:05 Darlie Routier ...who would do this ...who would do this...

03:13:09 Darin Routier ...(unintelligible)...

03:14:26 911 Operator #1 ...(sounds of typing on a computer keyboard)...

03:16:08 911 Operator #1 ...ma'am ...how old are your boys...

03:18:20 Darin Routier ...what...

03:19:03 911 Operator #1 ...how old are your boys...

03:20:04 RADIO ...(unintelligible)...

03:20:21 911 Operator #1 ...no...

03:21:01 Darlie Routier ...seven and five...
03:22:17 911 Operator #1 ...ok...
03:23:08 Darlie Routier ...oh my God ...oh my God ...oh ...he's dead...
03:29:02 911 Operator #1 ...calm down ...can you...
03:29:03 Darlie Routier ...oh God ...Devon no ...oh my God...
03:30:27 SOUND ...(dog barking)...
03:35:02 911 Operator #1 ...is your name Darlie...
03:36:11 Darlie Routier ...yes...
03:36:26 911 Operator #1 ...this is her...
03:37:09 911 Operator #1 ...is your husband's name Darin...
03:38:22 Darlie Routier ...yes ...please hurry ...God they're taking forever...
03:41:20 911 Operator #1 ...there's nobody in your house ...there was ...was...
03:44:05 911 Operator #1 ...you don't know who did this...

It was at this time that the first Officer David Waddell arrived on the scene.

Officer Waddell parked his patrol car in front of the Routier's home at the curve in the street.

The star indicates where Officer Waddell parked his patrol car.

When Officer Waddell exited his vehicle he saw Darrin running out of the front door, and across the yard.

Darin was saying something as he approached Waddell, but at that time he didn't know what it was.

Not knowing who this man was approaching him the officer drew his gun.

He hollered at him to stop, and then walked over and met him, in front of the fountain in front of the house.

Darin told him that his kids had been stabbed and that they were dying. Darin then turned and ran back into the house and Officer Waddell followed him inside.

When Officer Waddell entered the house he could see Darlie at the end of the entrance hallway standing in the kitchen.

Officer Waddell stood in the hallway for a moment and noticed some blood on the floor. He then continued into the house being sure not to step in it and disturb any of the blood evidence on the floor.

Darin Routier had gone back across the living room, to where Devon was still lying.

At this time Darlie, who appeared to be upset and hysterical, was still in the kitchen holding a greenish-colored towel over her neck with one hand and talking on the cordless phone with the other.

The question that many people have is, "If Darlie was bringing towels to put on the boy's backs, then why wasn't she still doing it when the officer entered the house? And if Darin was giving aid to the boys up until the police officer arrived and he went outside, why didn't she feel the need to help the boys and pick up where Darin left off when he left the house to meet the officer?"

AT THIS POINT THE FIRST POLICE OFFICER DAVID WADDELL IS IN THE HOUSE WITH DARLIE AND DARIN.

DARLIE DOES NOT HANG UP THE PHONE AS SOON AS THE POLICE ARRIVE SO WE CAN HEAR THE INTERACTION BETWEEN DARLIE AND THE RESPONDING OFFICER.

AT THE SAME TIME SHE IS STILL HAVING THE CONVERSATION WITH THE 911 COMMUNICATIONS OFFICER SO THERE IS SOME CONFUSION AS TO WHO SHE IS TALKING TO AND WHAT QUESTIONS SHE IS GIVING ANSWERS TO.

03:45:19 Officer David Waddell ...look for a rag...

WHY WOULD THE OFFICER HAVE TO TELL DARLIE TO LOOK FOR A RAG IF SHE WAS SUPPOSEDLY ALREADY TAKING WET TOWELS TO THE BOYS AS DARIN AND DARLIE CLAIMED IN THEIR TRIAL TESTIMONY?

03:46:11 Darlie Routier ...they killed our babies...
03:48:03 Officer David Waddell ...lay down ...ok ...just sit down ...(unintelligible)

03:51:11 911 Operator #1 ...(sounds of typing on a computer keyboard)...
03:52:13 Darlie Routier ...no ...he ran out ...uh ...they ran out in the garage ...I was sleeping...

She goes from, "he ran out" to "they ran out in the garage." And for some reason, she adds in the information that she was sleeping.

03:54:09 911 Operator #1 ...(unintelligible)...
03:56:19 Darlie Routier ...my babies over here already cut ...can I (unintelligible)...
03:59:29 Darin Routier ...(unintelligible) phone is right there...
04:01:28 Darlie Routier ...(unintelligible)...
04:03:01 RADIO ...(unintelligible)...
04:05:02 Darlie Routier ...ya'll look out in the garage ...look out in the garage ...they left a knife laying on...
04:08:21 RADIO ...(unintelligible)...
04:09:19 911 Operator #1 ...there's a knife ...don't touch anything...
04:11:18 Darlie Routier ...I already touched it and picked it up...

The fact that she picked up the knife has been a major topic of discussion on the internet. I would believe that she would have picked up the knife to defend herself if she believed that the attacker may return.

04:12:05 RADIO ...10-4...
04:15:20 911 Operator #1 ...who's out there ...is anybody out there...
04:16:07 Officer David Waddell ...(unintelligible)...
04:17:06 Darlie Routier ...I don't know ...I was sleeping...
04:18:14 911 Operator #1 ...ok ma'am ...listen ...there's a police officer at your front door ...is your front door unlocked...
04:22:11 RADIO ...(unintelligible)...
04:22:15 Darlie Routier ...yes ma'am ...but where's the ambulance...
04:24:21 911 Operator #1 ...ok...
04:24:23 Darlie Routier ...they're barely breathing...
04:26:17 Darlie Routier ...if they don't get it here they're gonna be dead ...my God they're (unintelligible) ...hurry ...please hurry...
04:31:13 911 Operator #1 ...ok ...they're ...they're...
04:32:18 Officer David Waddell ...what about you...
04:33:06 911 Operator #1 ...is 82 out on Eagle...
04:34:18 Darlie Routier ...huh...
04:35:12 Darin Routier ...they took (unintelligible) ...they ran (unintelligible)...

Two times in one sentence she reverts back to "they".

88

04:36:28 911 Operator #2 ...(unintelligible)...

04:37:08 Darlie Routier ...we're at Eagle ...5801 Eagle ...my God and hurry...

04:41:03 RADIO ...(unintelligible)...

04:41:22 911 Operator #1 ...82 ...are you out...

04:42:25 Officer David Waddell ...nothing's gone Mrs. Routier...

04:44:10 Darlie Routier ...oh my God ...oh my God ...why would they do this...

04:48:03 RADIO ...(unintelligible) to advise (unintelligible) 200...

04:50:18 Officer David Waddell ...(unintelligible) the problem Mrs. Routier...

04:50:21 911 Operator #1 ...what'd he say...

04:51:29 Darlie Routier ...why would they do this...

04:53:08 Darlie Routier ...I'm (unintelligible)...

04:54:07 911 Operator #1 ...ok ...listen ma'am ...need to ...need to let the officers in the front door ...ok...

04:59:11 Darlie Routier ...what...

05:00:04 911 Operator #1 ...ma'am..

05:00:22 Darlie Routier ...what ...what...

05:01:15 911 Operator #1 ...need to let the police officers in the front door...

05:04:21 Darlie Routier ...(unintelligible) his knife was lying over there and I already picked it up...

05:08:19 911 Operator #1 ...ok ...it's alright ...it's ok...

To many people, the following comment is the "Magic Bullet" of the 911 call.
05:09:20 Darlie Routier ...God ...I bet if we could have gotten the prints maybe ...maybe...

Darlie is making this statement as if she already knows that there are not going to be anyone else's prints on that knife except for hers. What she doesn't realize is that even if she did pick up the knife it would not make any other prints disappear. The worst-case scenario would be that she picked the knife up in the same fashion as someone else and the prints would just be smeared together, which did not happen.

05:13:18 Police Officer ...(unintelligible)...
05:14:18 RADIO ...82 ...we'll be (unintelligible)...
05:17:12 Darlie Routier ...ok ...it'll be...
05:18:08 911 Operator #1 ...ma'am ...hang on ...hang on a second...
05:19:09 Darlie Routier ...somebody who did it intentionally walked in here and did it Darin...

Why would she be making this statement to Darin? What made her feel that she needed to clarify this to him?

05:20:19 911 Operator #1 ...82 ...10-9...
05:21:23 RADIO ...(unintelligible)...
05:22:28 911 Operator #1 ...received...
05:23:05 Darlie Routier ...there's nothing

touched...
05:24:12 911 Operator #1 ...ok ma'am...
05:25:13 Darlie Routier ...there's nothing touched...
05:26:20 RADIO ...(unintelligible)...
05:28:00 Darlie Routier ...oh my God...
05:29:08 Police Officer ...(unintelligible)...
05:29:23 RADIO ...received...
05:31:19 RADIO ...(unintelligible)...
05:33:25 911 Operator #1 ...ma'am ...is the police officer there...
05:35:14 Darlie Routier ...yes (unintelligible)...
05:35:23 911 Operator #1 ...ok ...go talk to him ...ok...
05:38:03 RADIO ...(unintelligible)...

While Officer Waddell waited for backup to arrive he instructed Darlie to get some towels and put them on Devon's back to try to stop his bleeding.

However, instead of helping her son as the officer said, she stayed in the same place she was and told repeated top Officer Waddell that the attacker was still in the garage.

For years, Darlie's supporters have claimed that there were "bloody towels all over the place."

They claim that Darlie had been taking the towels to her boys in an attempt to save their lives.

91

However, it is a known fact that there were not "bloody towels all over the place."

Other than the towel that was found by Devon, there were only four towels inside the house with blood on them.

Two of these towels had only Darlie's blood on them.

The other two, found in the hallway far from both of the boys, were tested and the results were inconclusive. But from their location it common sense that they were never used to save either boy.

Not knowing where the attacker was located, Officer Waddell knew that he couldn't leave Darlie and Darin alone, so he walked halfway through the kitchen, stepping over the broken wine glass on the floor, and tried to look into the garage to see if he could see anyone.

The officer couldn't see into the garage from the kitchen area, and not wanting to leave Darlie and Darin alone with the suspect loose in the house somewhere, he chose to wait until backup arrived to search the garage area.

While Office Waddell was trying to get a glimpse into the garage, Darin was in the living room with Devon, and Darlie remained at the sink area not trying to assist Darin in saving her son's life.

When Officer Waddell returns from trying to look in the garage Darlie tells him that she had got into a fight with the man that broke into the house.

She said that she fought with him at the end of the bar and that he ran across the kitchen towards the garage.

As the officer was talking to Darlie, he could see that Damon was lying on the floor on his stomach, on his left side of his face and he was looking up at both of them with his eyes open making a gasping-type noise like he was trying to breathe.

At that point, Officer Waddell still didn't know where the suspect was.

He thought he could still be in the garage and he didn't know if there could have been a second person still in the house.

So he had to position himself between the victims and the rest of the house until he could get another officer to help clear the house.

He also knew that he couldn't go over to help Damon and have a suspect come in the room and stab him too, so he instructed Darlie to get some towels and put them on his back to try to stop the bleeding.

But rather than getting the towels and try to help save her son's life, she just kept telling the officer that when she chased the suspect across the kitchen, that he had dropped the knife and that she had picked up the knife and brought it back and set it on the counter.

And instead of focusing on her dying son, she tells the officer that she thought she had messed up the fingerprints.

The Crime Scene

Sergeant Matt Walling arrived on the scene right behind the first ambulance.

The two paramedics, Jack Kolbye and Brian Koschak stayed inside the ambulance because they were informed that the emergency at the home was a possible stabbing and the procedure is to wait for the police to let them know that the scene is clear before entering.

Sergeant Walling entered the Routier's house and Officer Waddell briefed him on what happened and told him that the suspect was probably still in the house somewhere, most likely in the garage.

The two officers then went to the garage to check and see if anybody was in there.

Sergeant Walling noticed that there was blood on the door and around the door handle.

Sergeant Walling opened the door that led into the garage. There were no lights on in the garage and it was dark, so he scanned the garage with his flashlight. And, he stepped in just a couple of feet and went to the left and Officer Waddell stuck his head into the doorway and looked to the right.

NOTE: THE DOOR BETWEEN THE KITCHEN AND THE UTILITY ROOM WAS OPEN AND THE DOOR LEADING INTO THE GARAGE WAS CLOSED.

IF THE DOOR LEADING TO THE GARAGE WAS CLOSED, THEN THAT WOULD MEAN THAT THE KILLER FLED AND CLOSED THE DOOR BEHIND HIM.

IT IS VERY UNLIKELY THAT A PERSON JUST BUTCHERED TWO CHILDREN, ATTACKED THEIR MOTHER WHO WAS NOW RIGHT BEHIND HIM AND HE STOPS HIS ATTEMPT TO FLEE TO CLOSE THE DOOR BEHIND HIM.

Sergeant Walling took only one step into the garage and looked to the left and informed Officer Waddell that he saw a screen that had been cut.

After searching the garage and not finding anyone, and with the window being cut, Sergeant Walling assumed that the attacker must have had possibly left out that way.

Sergeant Walling knew that he had to get around to the backyard as quick as he could to continue searching for the attacker.

Because the house still wasn't secured at that time, and knowing that another officer was coming to meet Sergeant Walling, Officer Waddell went back to the area where Darin and Darlie were located.

When he returned to where Darin and Darlie were located, Darlie was in the same location she was at when he left to search the garage area, and there was still no towel placed on Damon's back.

Less than two minutes after arriving at the crime scene, Sergeant Walling exited the house to go to the backyard.

He immediately went to the driver's side door of the ambulance and told Kolbe, "You have two children inside. You're going to need some more help. Go on in."

Paramedic Koschak got on the radio and called for an additional engine, fire truck, and ambulance while Jack Kolbye grabbed the medical kit out of the side compartment of the ambulance and proceeded inside.

After making the radio call for additional help, Brian Koschak followed Kolbye inside.

When the paramedics entered the home they made their way to the kitchen area where they saw Officer Waddell and Darlie, holding a towel on her neck, in the kitchen area standing near the bar, and Darin in the middle of the living room.

As soon as Kolbye looked at Officer Waddell, he gave Kolbye a nod indicating the direction Just to Kolbye's left, where Damon was lying face down on the floor.

Kolbye quickly went to Damon and examined his backside briefly for any injuries, and then rolled him over so that he would be facing face up.

Paramedic Kolbye said that when he rolled Damon over, he gasped for air and that was the final time that he breathed.

Damon's eyes were still open and Kolbye seen that there was still light of life in those eyes. However, that life slowly faded.

While Kolbye was trying to save Damon's life Paramedic Koschak immediately went to try and save Devon in the living room.

At this point, help has arrived, and are actively working to save the two boy's lives. But surprisingly, Darlie doesn't ask anyone about the condition of her children.

This is odd as all she did on the 911 call is say that her babies were dying.

About the time Sergeant Walling was coming around into the driveway from the front of the house, Officer Darcel Moore had pulled up.

Sergeant Walling motioned to him to follow him into the backyard to help search for the suspected killer.

As Sergeant Walling and Officer D. Moore searched the backyard the paramedics were inside attempting to save the two boy's lives.

Sergeant Walling and Officer D. Moore went to the gate that was next to the garage door that led into the backyard.

The first thing that Sergeant Walling noticed is that the gate was closed.

The gate was latched but there was not a lock on it.

Sergeant Walling lifted the latch and used the handle to push it open.

The gate wouldn't open when he first pushed on it so he had to use his foot at the bottom of the gate to apply pressure and ended up shoving it open. As he opened the gate the bottom was dragging on the ground making it difficult to open.

NOTE: SERGEANT WALLING TESTIFIED THAT THE GATE LEADING TO THE BACKYARD WAS CLOSED AND LATCHED. AND THAT HE HAD TO USE FORCE TO PUSH THE GATE OPEN WITH HIS FOOT

BECAUSE IT DRAGGED ON THE GROUND AS IT OPENED.

THE FACT THAT DARIN SAID THAT HE HAD FIXED THE GATE THE AFTERNOON PRIOR IS ONE ISSUE THAT WE NOTICE HERE.

BUT THE BIGGER ISSUE IS THIS: WHY DID THE KILLER TAKE THE TIME AS HE FLED A CRIME SCENE WHERE HE HAD JUST ATTACKED 3 PEOPLE AND WAS BEING CHASED BY DARLIE, TAKE THE TIME TO STOP HIS RUNNING AND CLOSE THE GATE BEHIND HIM?

THIS GATE RUBBED THE GROUND SO IT WAS NOT LIKE THE GATE JUST SWUNG CLOSED BY ITSELF AFTER THE KILLER FLED THROUGH IT; IT HAD TO BE FORCEFULLY PULLED CLOSED.

IT IS VERY UNLIKELY THAT THE KILLER TOOK THE TIME TO MAKE SURE THAT THE GATE WAS CLOSED AS HE FLED FROM THE CRIME SCENE!

When Sergeant Walling first entered the backyard he saw that there was a spa house in the opposite corner of the yard.

There were no outside lights on when he entered the backyard.

After getting his bearings on where the window was that had been cut in the garage, he went into the backyard and started to search, looking around for things that were covered by his view.

He went around past the spa house and checked on the side of it. Looked around the corner of the yard, to where it wraps back around toward the front yard.

After checking the area he approached the spa house and when he was walking in front of the spa house the motion sensor light that was mounted on the spa house came on. He then entered the spa house, and did a search, and found nobody inside.

While in the backyard examining the area around the window with the cut screen, Sergeant Walling could see the reflection from the TV through the blinds, through the slats.

NOTE: AT THIS TIME THE MOTION LIGHT IS ON IN THE BACKYARD AND SERGEANT WALLING STILL NOTICES THE GLARE COMING FROM THE TELEVISION INSIDE OF THE HOUSE. THIS WOULD MEAN THAT THE KILLER WOULD ALSO HAVE SEEN THE GLARE FROM THE TELEVISION COMING THROUGH THE BLINDS. THIS WOULD HAVE INDICATED THAT THE HOUSE WAS OCCUPIED.

MANY OF DARLIE'S SUPPORTERS CLAIM THAT THE PERSON WHO BROKE INTO THE HOUSE THAT NIGHT THOUGHT THE HOUSE

WAS EMPTY AND WAS ONLY GOING IN TO STEAL VALUABLES. WE CAN NOW SEE THAT WHOEVER ENTERED THE HOUSE DID KNOW THAT SOMEONE WAS INSIDE THE HOME.

After searching the backyard, Sergeant Walling instructed Officer Moore to start a search of the neighborhood for suspects.

Sergeant Walling then went back around to the front of the Routier's house and came back inside.

There was so much screaming, and so much anguish in the house at that time, that Paramedic Kolbye felt that he could help Damon better he got him out to the ambulance.

Sadly, when Paramedic Koschak got to Devon, He had no pulse and was not breathing. And at that point, there was nothing that he could do for him.

He then went to give aid to Darlie who was still inside the house and standing next to the kitchen bar with Officer Waddell.

Kolbye was only in the Routier's house about two minutes when he looked up and could tell that Paramedic Koschak was going to be busy and that he wasn't going to be able to assist him.

Damon was not breathing and there was no pulse. So Kolbye decided to pick Damon up and carry him out to the ambulance where the advanced life support that he would need be.

Kolbye needed to get Damon hooked up to an EKG monitor as soon as possible.

He carried Damon, face-up, in his arms.

Kolbye noticed that Damon wasn't bleeding as he carried him out to the ambulance.

When he stopped and opened the back of the ambulance he had to prop Damon on his chest with his knee to free an arm to open the rear door.

And he had very little blood on him, only what would have rubbed off of his clothes on to him.

This is a common occurrence with victims whose heart has stopped pumping blood. With no heartbeat, blood will not flow through the veins and exit much through open wounds.

When they got into the ambulance he continued CPR, which he had started inside the house before he carried him out.

The fire department's engine company arrived shortly after Damon was put in the ambulance, and

Kolbye saw that Paramedic Coleman was available, so he asked him to assist him.

Kolbye and Paramedic Coleman continued working on Damon with the advanced life support in the back of the ambulance probably 15 minutes before they transported him to Baylor University Medical Center in Dallas.

Baylor University Medical Center in Dallas was a 15-minute drive from Eagle Drive.

Back inside the Routier's house, Sergeant Walling knew that the rest of the house had to be cleared, so he and Officer Waddell went and searched the upstairs.

After a thorough search of the second floor, the only person they found was 8-month old Drake standing up in his crib just looking over the rail in the master bedroom.

Officer Waddell went over and checked the infant to see if it was injured.

When it was determined that Drake had no injuries, the officers decided to leave Drake there in his crib seeing that the second floor was cleared and it was determined to be a safe place for the child.

The paramedic removed the rag from Darlie's neck and noticed a large laceration to her neck area, and also a laceration to her right arm.

He knew that he had to get Darlie out of the house, so he asked her to come with him to the front porch.

Once they were out on the front porch, Paramedic Koschak began assessing her injuries again.

He quickly determined that she was not suffering from shock and he and a second Paramedic named Larry Byford started to bandage the wounds on her neck and arm.

As the two officers walked down the stairs towards the first floor they noticed the Routier's neighbor, Karen was in the entryway and Darlie was sitting on the front porch while the paramedics were attending to her wounds.

They placed gauze over her neck and arm wounds.

NOTE: DARLIE'S SUPPORTERS CLAIM THAT HER WOUNDS THAT NIGHT WAS LIFE THREATENING AND SOME HAVE EVEN GONE TO THE EXTENT TO SAY THAT SHE WAS ALMOST DECAPITATED AND KILLED.

IF THAT WAS THE CASE THE PARAMEDICS WOULD HAVE TAKEN HER STRAIGHT TO AN AMBULANCE AND RUSHED HER TO THE HOSPITAL. BUT HER WOUNDS WERE "NOT LIFE-THREATENING" SO THEY JUST TENDED TO HER WOUNDS AS SHE SAT ON THE FRONT STEPS.

Sergeant Walling went outside and started finding out the locations of the other responding officers that he called for and started assigning perimeter areas for them to set up and different areas for them to drive in an attempt to locate the suspect and started stringing up crime scene tape across the street.

At this point, Sergeant Walling also notified his lieutenant and attempted to arrange for a K-9 unit and a helicopter search.

The K-9 unit was quickly dispatched to the crime scene.

However, when he contacted the Texas Department of Public Service helicopter division he was told that a helicopter would not be successful for a night search in that type of neighborhood.

At this time the paramedics have Darlie sitting on the front porch of the house.

(This goes to the point that her wounds were not life-threatening as they would have immediately taken her to the hospital if her wounds were very serious)

Sergeant Walling went up and asked Darlie if she could tell him what happened.

Her response to Sergeant Walling was that she was asleep on the couch and that she had been awakened when she felt somebody standing over her. She told him that she realized that she had been stabbed.

She said that when she woke up, the person was standing over her, and that she was lying on the couch, and that she began struggling with the person on the couch. And that they had run out through the kitchen door into the garage.

This conversation between Sergeant Walling and Darlie was within the first 10-minutes of him arriving on the scene so her memories of the events were fresh in her mind.

Even though her wounds did not appear to be life-threatening the paramedics knew that they had to take her to the hospital.

A stretcher was brought up to the front porch and they walked her to the stretcher and she got up onto it. She was then taken to the ambulance.

Once they got into the ambulance the paramedics started their routine procedure of evaluating the patient and asking Darlie about her medical history and any medications she may be taking.

She did say that she was taking weight loss medication.

After the paramedic had cut Darlie's tee-shirt off, he realized that he had taped her necklace under the bandage.

One of the paramedics tried to move it just a little bit, but it irritated her, and so he left it alone.

Darlie was then transported to Baylor University Medical Center in Dallas just after 3:00 a.m. where Damon had just been rushed to.

I want to point out a fact here for all of the Darlie supporters.

Had her wounds been as life-threatening as you suggest, then why did the paramedics wait thirty minutes from the time she hung up with the 911 operator to take her to the hospital if her wounds were life-threatening?

I'll tell you exactly why they did not rush her to the hospital. Darlie's wounds were not life-threatening!

Darin had a neighbor Terry Neil drive him to the hospital to be with Darlie, and Karen Neil, the neighbor's wife, stayed behind to take care of the Routier's youngest son Drake.

As the ambulances pulled away from the curb transporting Damon and Darlie to the hospital, more law enforcement officers were en route to the crime scene.

Neighbors began coming out of their homes and standing on their lawns trying to get a glimpse of the activity surrounding the Routier's home.

NOTE: THERE HAVE BEEN NUMEROUS CLAIMS ABOUT A BLACK VEHICLE SPEEDING AWAY FROM THE SCENE SOON AFTER THE POLICE ARRIVED. YES, THERE WAS A DARK VEHICLE THAT LEFT THE AREA SHORTLY AFTER THE POLICE ARRIVED.

HERE IS THE STORY OF THAT VEHICLE.

While Sergeant Walling was on his radio in the front yard a dark-colored Sedan came around from the side of the house towards the front of the house.

When he noticed it he stepped out in the street and stopped the vehicle.

Inside the vehicle were four occupants. He drew his weapon and ordered the two white males, one black male, and one female passenger out of the car at gunpoint.

Once he had the occupants of the vehicle out of the car he ordered them to place their hands on the hood of the car so that he could check them for weapons and identify them.

The description of the man that he was looking for was a white male wearing a dark-colored ball cap, a black shirt, and blue jeans.

After he checked them for weapons he checked the interior of the vehicle for anything relating to this crime.

After searching their vehicle and checking each one of their clothing and shoes for any signs of blood. He also made them show him their hands, front and back.

He soon determined that they were not involved in the crime and released them.

He then made a few more calls for crime scene technicians while Officer Waddell went to the front door and waited for the paramedics to come out.

At about 2:45 the paramedics were leaving the house, Officer Waddell noticed one of them was carrying Drake downstairs and they were all going outside.

Drake was then given to Karen Neal to take across the street to her house.

After the ambulance left the scene with Darlie heading to the hospital, Paramedic Koschak went across the street to Karen Neal's home to evaluate the Routier's youngest son Drake for any injuries.

After evaluating Drake, Koschak went back to the Routier's home to retrieve his medical emergency equipment and to do one more evaluation of his first victim, Devon, whose lifeless body was still on the living room floor.

When Koschak exited the Routier's home for the last time, he told Officer Waddell that there was nothing more that he could do for Devon.

Officer Waddell remained at the entrance door to secure the crime scene. The only person left inside of the Routier's house was Devon, whose lifeless body was still lying on the living room floor.

Officer Waddell stayed at the front door until around 3:00 am when Officer Steve Wade relieved him.

Officer Waddell then went with Garland K-9 Officer Griffith and his dog for about 25 minutes, around the neighborhood, up and down the alleys, and across front yards to help search the area for any clues and to try and find the killer.

When Officer Waddell returned to the Routier's home, he was instructed to stay in the alley and stop anybody who came down the alley and identify them and asks if they had heard anything out of the ordinary for that night.

About 6:00 a.m. Sergeant Walling, Officer David Mayne, and the Routier's neighbor Karen Neal went into the house to remove the Routier's small dog from the second-floor landing.

Officer Waddell stayed in the alley behind the Routier's home till about 7:00 or 8:00 in the morning.

During that time he only stopped one vehicle that was driven by a young woman on her way to work.

Once he was relieved from his post behind the house he went back to the police station to write his report until about 11:00 that morning.

NOTE: Officer Waddell returned to the police station during his next shift to fill out a Supplemental Offense Report.

A Supplemental Offense Report is a report that is made to add information to the case notes that the officer had remembered or thought was significant to the case after he had already written and submitted their original report.

Many of Darlie's supporters claim that this Supplemental Offense Report was not commonly done and that it was only written to make Darlie look guilty.

As a police officer myself, I have written many Supplemental Offense Reports myself when something jarred my memory of events that I may have not thought were important to the case when the original report was written.

When Officer Waddell learned that Darlie was a suspect he may have felt that her actions that morning of not trying to give any type of aid to her dying children was reason to write a Supplemental Offense Report.

I will also add that if Officer Waddell was lying at the time that he wrote his second report, how did the physical evidence at the scene supported his statement of Darlie not running through the kitchen with wet towels?

Officers were dispatched to search the surrounding area for anything or anyone that seemed out of place.

One of the officers found a discarded sock 75 yards up the alley from the Routier's home.

The sock was collected as evidence and sent to Gene Screen which is a company that performs DNA identity testing.

The investigators felt that at the time it was a good idea not to let the Routiers know that the sock was discovered until it could be ruled to either belong to the Routiers or not.

I want to take a moment to discuss the 75-yard distance from the Routier's home to where the sock was located.

Many of Darlie's supporters claim that this is an extremely far distance from the Routier's home.

The circle in the bottom right of the photo shows the location of the drain located in front of the Routier's home. The star on the bottom left shows the location where the sock was discovered.

As you can see the location is just two houses down from the Routier's home. It is not a very far distance.

These photos are looking at where the sock was found and the Routier's property.

To give you an idea of how far 75 yards is.

The distance between the two entrances of a Wal-Mart Supercenter is about 75 yards. And I can walk that distance in less than a minute.

So a woman can sprint from her home to where the sock was located and back to her house in a very short amount of time.

It was later determined with DNA testing that the sock did come from the Routier's home.

The sock was determined to have belonged to Darin.

The DNA testing lab discovered a total of six small stains on the sock. Two of those stains came from Damon and three came from Devon.

One of the stains they were not able to get DNA from.

Darlie's DNA was also discovered in the toe of the sock.

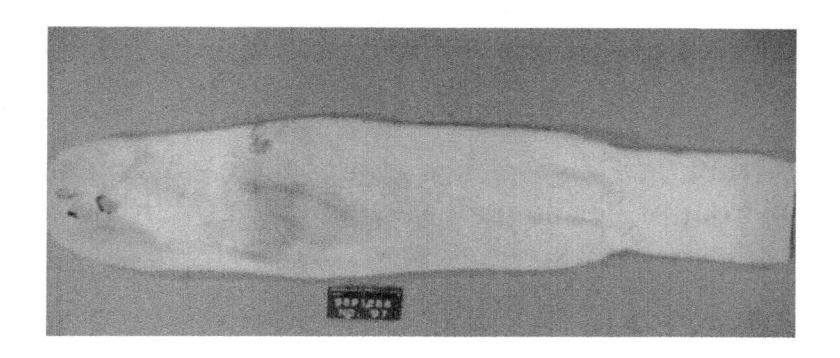

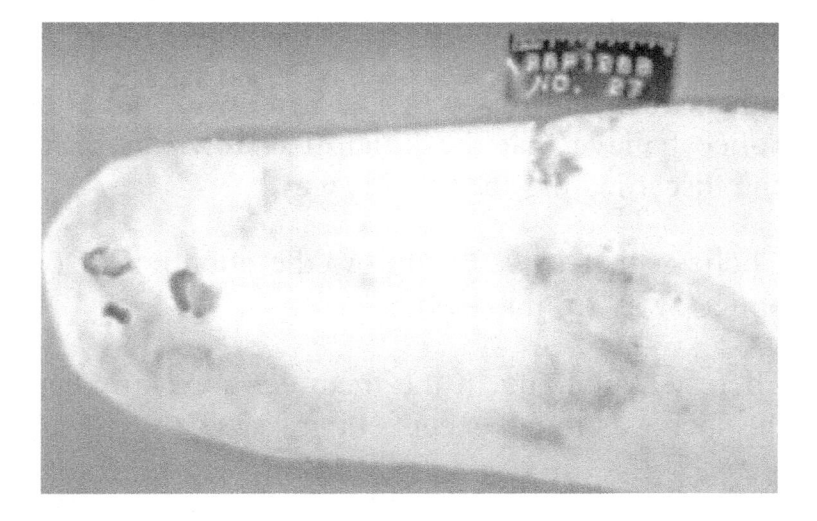

I also want to point out that the sock was only 75 yards down the alley from the Routier's house.

Many people feel that Darlie was trying to dispose of the sock that she wore on her hand when stabbing her boys.

That she went down the alley and threw the sock towards the drain in the road but missed and did not realize this and the sock was left out for the police to discover.

I doubt that this was her goal as there was a drain in front of her home that would have been closer for her to dispose of the sock.

Also, a person would have to be very close to the drain opening to throw an item as light as a sock down. So she would have known that the sock did not go into the drain if that was her plan.

Others feel that this was just a ploy to make the police believe that the killer fled down the alley and discarded the sock on his way.

I believe that it was to throw the attention of the police away from herself.

There was nothing in the trash can next to where the sock was found except cut grass.

Also, the garbage can had a lid on it. So if the intention was to hide the evidence from the police, she would have had to have lifted the lid before tossing anything into it.

That was not done and the sock was left out to be found.

She would later accuse the homeowner of that home of the killings and maybe she was planting the sock to frame him or to make the police focus their attention on him.

Darlie in the Hospital

Here is the timeline of Darlie's first three hours in the hospital according to the doctor and nurse's reports.

This timeline will clarify the amount of time Darlie spent in the emergency room in the emergency room.

3:25 a.m.: Darlie arrives in the emergency room.

3:40 a.m.: Darlie is brought into the operating room.

3:50 a.m.: Examination begins to get a closer look at her neck wound.

4:35 a.m.: Examination on Darlie's neck wound ends; (According to her medical chart, the cleansing, evaluation, and closing procedure took 49 minutes not 2 hours as most of Darlie's supporters claim and was considered "an outpatient procedure.") surgeons then begin to tend to Darlie's remaining wounds.

4:49 a.m.: Tending to her remaining wounds end.

5:00 a.m.: Anesthesia ends.

6:00 a.m.: ICU nurse gives Darlie 25 mg. of Demerol to help with her pain.

6:11 a.m.: Rowlett P.D. detectives Chris Frosch and James Patterson begin the first police interview of Darlie at the hospital.

Here are the details of her stay at the hospital.

Darlie arrived at Baylor University Medical Center's emergency room in Dallas at 3:25 that morning.

When she arrived at the hospital her vital signs were stable. She was awake and alert and responsive. She was also aware of everything going on around her.

And when she was asked, she stated that she had not lost consciousness.

One of the first questions that a doctor would ask a patient with a severe cut is, "how did this happen?"

This is asked because the medical staff needs to know if the wounds were caused by a knife, scissors, a piece of glass, or some other object.

Most patients would simply say that they were cut or even stabbed.

However, Darlie felt that it was necessary to go into detail about who stabbed her.

She told the doctor treating her that it was a white male in a baseball cap.

And she even felt the need to tell him that she only saw him from the back.

Darlie was only in the emergency room for thirteen minutes.

During this time she had enough sense to tell the doctor the full description of her attacker, but yet not one time did she ask about the condition of her son who she knows was already taken to the hospital.

I guess the condition of her son wasn't a top priority at the time.

As we go forward to discuss the time that Darlie was in the hospital, I want to point out that 99% of what Darlie supports claim are lies!

Darlie was not almost dead when she arrived at Baylor.

She was not almost decapitated as many have claimed.

She was not in any imminent danger of dying when she arrived.

The time that Darlie spent at Baylor and the testimony of the doctors who treated her will shine a light on the numerous lies that have been spread over the years.

First and foremost let's focus on her emergency surgery that many have claimed was the only thing that saved her life.

If you ever read any statements made by Darlie's family and her supporters they use the phrase, "the surgery performed on her neck" quite often.

What they fail to tell anyone is that the hospital's emergency room department divides the neck into three zones, and that is how they manage them.

Darlie's wound was considered a zone two injury.

In zone 2 injuries there is a better chance of the wound affecting a vital part of the neck. The most vital part of zone 2 of the neck is the jugular vein.

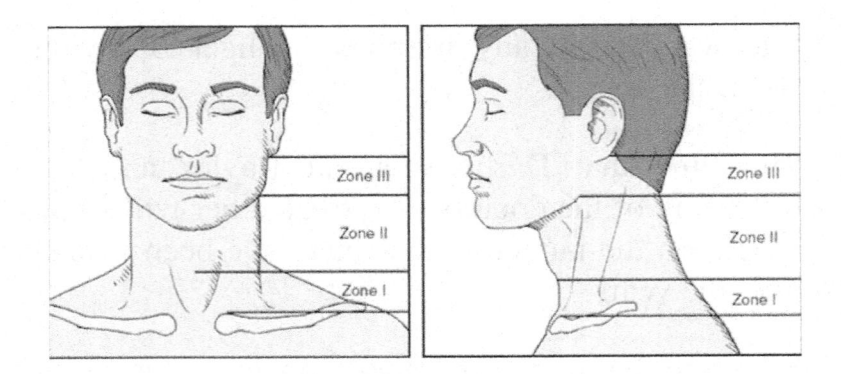

Darlie's neck wound was evaluated in the emergency department.

The necklace fell free once the bandage was removed in the emergency department and was not embedded in the wound like her supporters claimed over the years.

Some have gone to the extent of saying that yes the necklace was embedded and had to be removed during surgery because if it had been loose around Darlie's neck it would have been removed, along with all her other clothing when she was initially treated.

I guess common sense and the ability to read basic paramedic reports and Darlie's statements are not as important as trying to prove Darlie's innocence.

Darlie wrote in her statement: *I remember we got to the hospital and then them telling me they were taking me to surgery. They took off my necklace and put me to sleep.*

If the wound was in any other part of the neck the patient would normally be stitched up and observed for a while and then released to go home.

But, Darlie's wound was in the portion of the neck where the emergency room doctors didn't want to push and prod around.

Because they might disrupt a blood clot that's clogging a vessel, which means it's keeping it from bleeding.

And if the clot is disturbed it could make the situation worse.

So the decision to go to an operating room to do exploratory surgery to evaluate her neck wound was made in case something was loosened and made the situation life-threatening.

The decision to take Darlie to the operating room was not based on her condition.

It was solely based on the location of her wound and the need for the doctors to be in a better-suited environment in case anything changed in the condition of the bleeding.

Once Darlie was prepped for the exploratory surgery and placed under anesthesia the doctors examined her neck wound.

During the 45 minute procedure, they found several very small veins bleeding, which they tied off and the bleeding had stopped.

And then they just rinsed out the wound and looked around for any major vessel injury, an injury to her windpipe and esophagus, and they didn't see anything that concerned them.

Many of her supporters even claim that she could not have inflicted her wounds because the cut was within 2 to 3 millimeters of the carotid artery.

This does not prove that she didn't inflict the cut herself. It only proves that she is lucky that she didn't cut any deeper and sever her jugular vein and die.

Even the doctor described it as a superficial wound because it just penetrated the skin and the subcutaneous tissue, which is referred to as the fat, underlying the skin.

That was the extent of the neck injury.

While the doctors were examining her neck injury the other residents sewed up the wounds on her shoulder and her arm.

Some of the Darlie supporters claim that she couldn't have inflicted the wounds to her arm because the knife penetrated to the bone.

Again I have to say, this does not prove that she didn't inflict the cut herself. It only proves that she is unlucky that she cut deep enough to hit bone.

I will point out that nowhere in any of the Doctor's reports or testimony do they state that they removed her necklace from the neck wound.

This made-up story about the necklace being so far embedded in her neck that the doctors had to surgically remove it had to be made up by a total idiot who did not realize that this information can be verified.

Some of these people have even gone to the extent of saying that her necklace saved her life because it had a knick on it from where the killer's knife was stopped.

ARE YOU SERIOUS?

Anyone who believes that a full-grown man who had just brutally stabbed two children to the extent of severing internal organs did not have enough strength to push a knife blade past a woman's tiny necklace.

This theory does not make any sense at all. But it is another piece of fabricated facts that have been made up to create an illusion that Darlie just couldn't have killed her boys.

Almost all of Darlie's jewelry was purchased at a pawn shop; it was used jewelry. Who's to say that nick in the chain wasn't there when she purchased it?

Another crazy theory is that Darlie was so injured that the doctors had to admit her and put her in the Intensive Care Unit to recover.

This is another smoke and mirror tactic that her supporters use to deflect from the facts.

After Darlie was out of the operating room, Dr, Santos decided to put Darlie in the Intensive Care Unit because he knew what happened with the two boys and was afraid that all this might be a little too much for her.

He was concerned about Darlie's psychological state.

He was concerned that once she fully knew what had happened at her home that both children were dead, that she might be in a very precarious psychological state.

He also knew that there would be a lot of media wanting to speak to her, and he didn't want her disturbed.

So "NO", Darlie was not in the ICU because she was injured that badly. It was for her protection.

This photo of Darlie was taken just 8 days after the murders.

You can see how quickly her neck wound is healing.

If her neck wound had been as serious as her supporters claim, it would not have been healed in a matter of only 8 days.

Numerous medical personnel who worked at the hospital were subpoenaed to testify on Darlie's demeanor while she was hospitalized.

I am not going to comment on Darlie's demeanor as I know that each person grieves and deals with situations differently.

Maybe she didn't cry enough or show enough emotion concerning the fact that her boys were dying.

All I will say is that none of these nurses were in the hospital room with Darlie 24 hours a day and nobody can set the bar as to how a person is to show emotions.

So I will stand on my statement that a person's emotions or lack of emotion do not weigh on their guilt or innocence.

One thing that has a lot of people yelling "INNOCENT" is the wounds that Darlie had on her arms two days after she was released from the hospital.

Darlie's supporters claim that she received these wounds from the intruder either hitting her arms as she fought him or being grabbed as she was attacked.

Before we even go into these questions I want to point out a blatant lie that has been spread over the years that has been proven to be a lie.

One of the jurors claimed that the jury has never seen the photos of her injuries on her arms and if they did they would not have voted to convict her.

This juror is either blind, has a bad memory, or is just outright lying because Dr. Patrick Dillawn testified on January 9, 1997, just days after the start of the trial.

It was Darlie's defense lawyer Toby L. Shook who asked Dr. Patrick Dillawn, "Okay. Now, let me show you what's been marked as State's Exhibit 52-A. Do you recognize that as a photograph of Ms. Routier?"

Dr. Patrick Dillawn, "Yes"

Toby L. Shook, "Do you see her right arm there and the bruising on her right arm?"

Dr. Patrick Dillawn, "Yes."

Toby L. Shook, "What type of injury is that? What's that called"?

Dr. Patrick Dillawn, "That's what we would term medically a hematoma it's a large bruise."

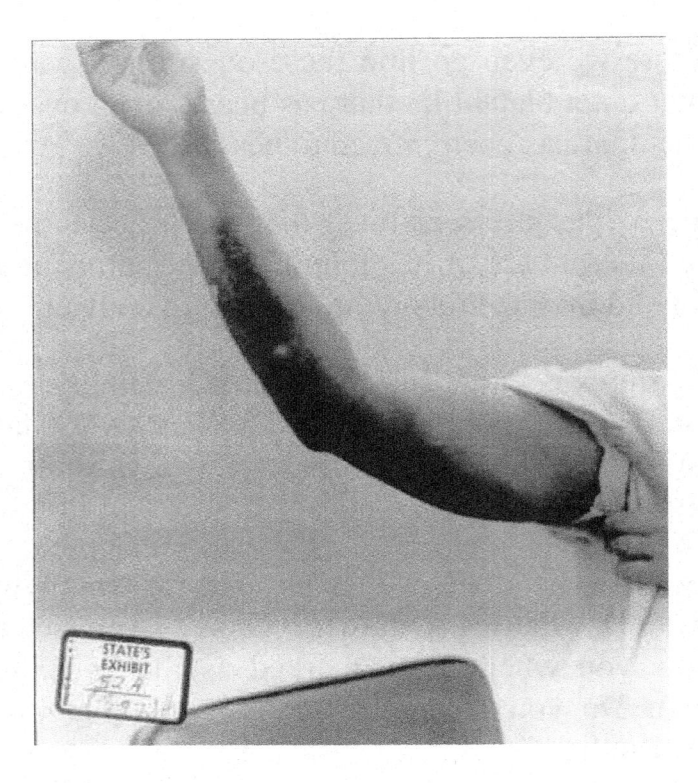

This is the picture known as State's Exhibit 52-A

But this wasn't the only photo shown to the jury on that day.

Toby L. Shook, "Okay. Let me show you some other photographs marked 52-G, 52-H, and 52-F. And let me ask you if you can recognize those photos.

Dr. Patrick Dillawn, "These appear to be Mrs. Routier in the intensive care unit. And they're photographs of her neck wound and her arm wounds."

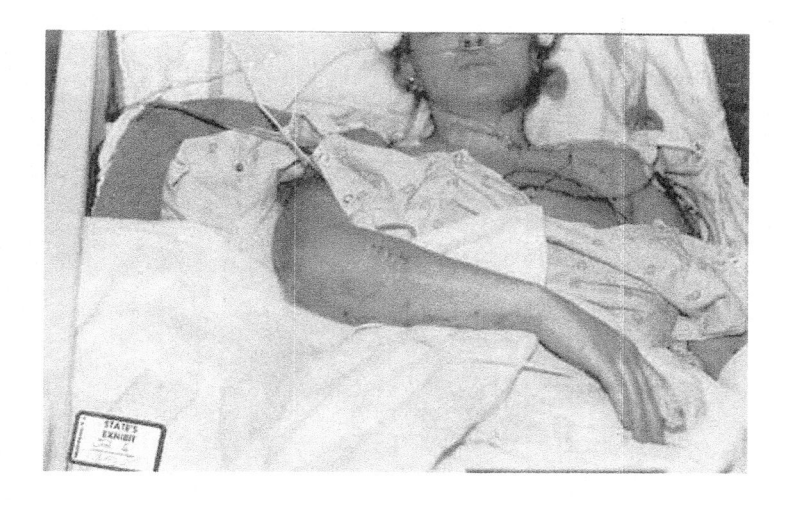

This is the picture known as State's Exhibit 52-G

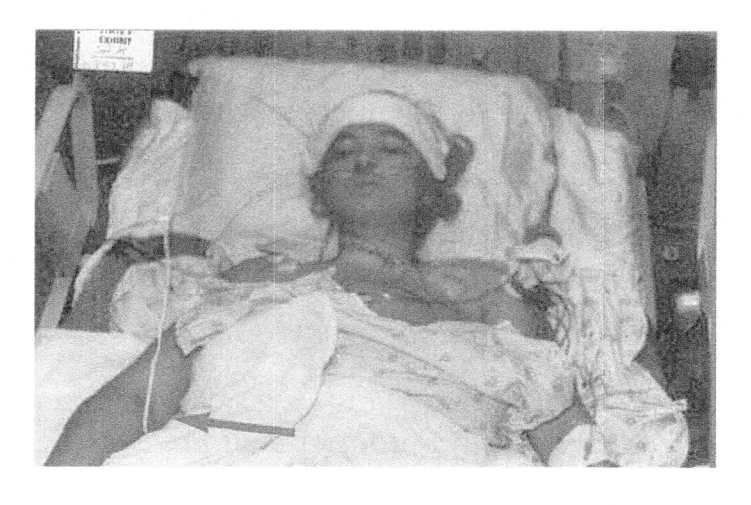

This is the picture known as State's Exhibit 52-H

If you look at where the arrow is pointing you will notice that there is no bruising whatsoever on Darlie's arm.

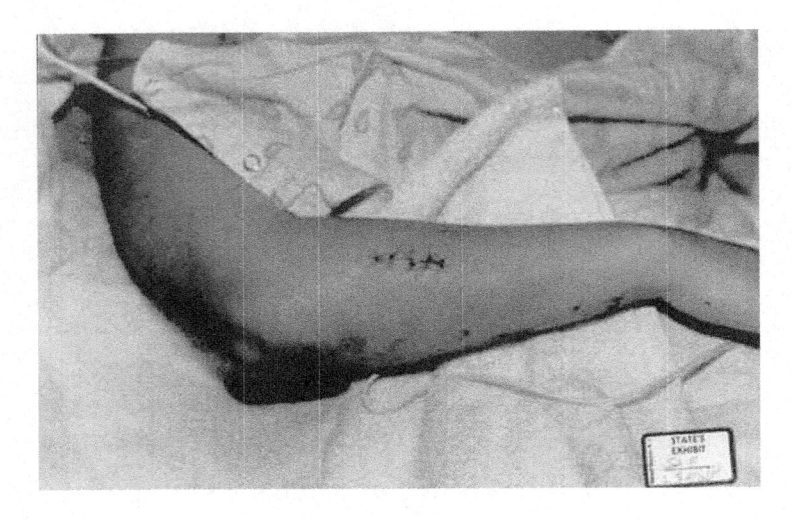

This is the picture known as State's Exhibit 52-F

Many people go to this picture to claim that they see bruising in the photo. But when you go online and enhance the size you will see that it is simply shadowing and that the dark area is also on the sheet below her arm.

So, if anyone ever tells you that the jury never saw the bruises on Darlie's arm. You can call them a liar and that you have proof of their lie.

Now we need to ask ourselves if the bruises on Darlie's arms came from her attacker or if they were self-inflicted.

Dr. Patrick Dillawn testified that these types of bruises are called a blunt injury, as in not something sharp

You can see these types of injuries from striking your hand against a hard object, like being in a car wreck and hitting the steering wheel, something in that nature.

He also stated that he never saw this bruising while Darlie was in the hospital. He said that would have been something that he would have looked for in his examination of her.

And if he had seen the bruising he would have wanted to x-ray her arm to check for any broken bones.

Dr. Patrick Dillawn visited Darlie every day from the morning of the 6th when she was admitted until the 8th when she was discharged.

And at no time did he see any evidence of this type of bruising.

He was asked during the trial if that injury, that blunt trauma, had occurred on June 6th, about 2:30 in the morning, 1996, would he have seen evidence of that injury on her right arm.

He answered that in his opinion, yes. This is a lot of blood, yes.

He was also asked if that type of wound would be caused by an I.V.

His answer was, No. He had never seen such a severe hematoma caused by an intravenous line.

So to go back to the juror who claimed that they did not know of any of the bruising to Darlie's arm we can see that this topic was covered in detail during Dr. Patrick Dillawn's testimony.

"YES." The jury did know about these bruises.

But where did Darlie's arm bruising come from?

Well first of all let's point out the fact that there is no bruising whatsoever on the top of her forearm or triceps. All of the bruising is underneath these areas.

Here are two pictures of her bruises to show the bruising better.

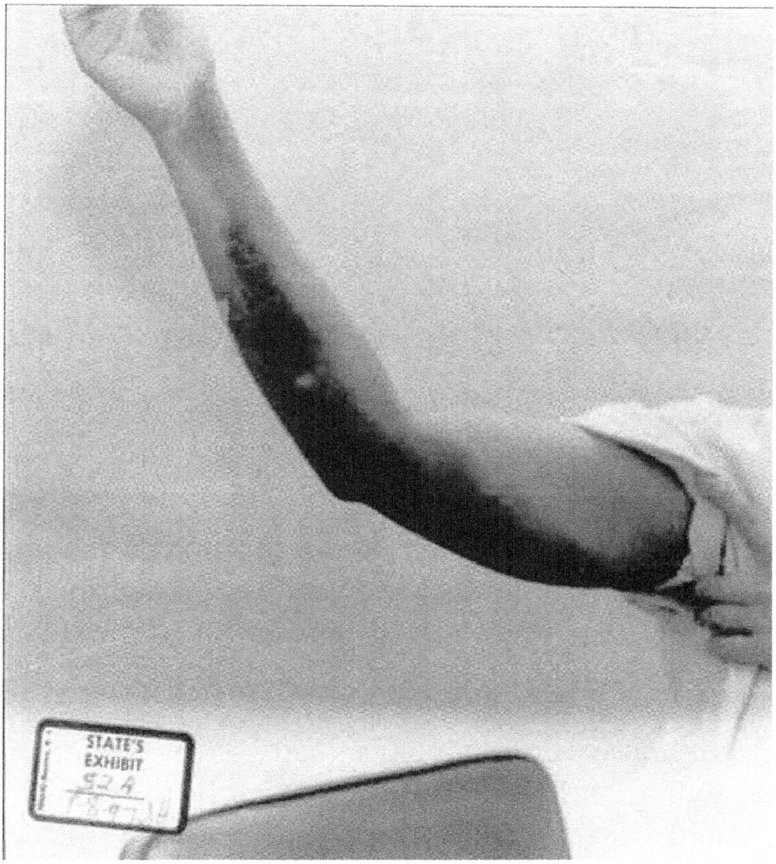
STATE'S
EXHIBIT
52A

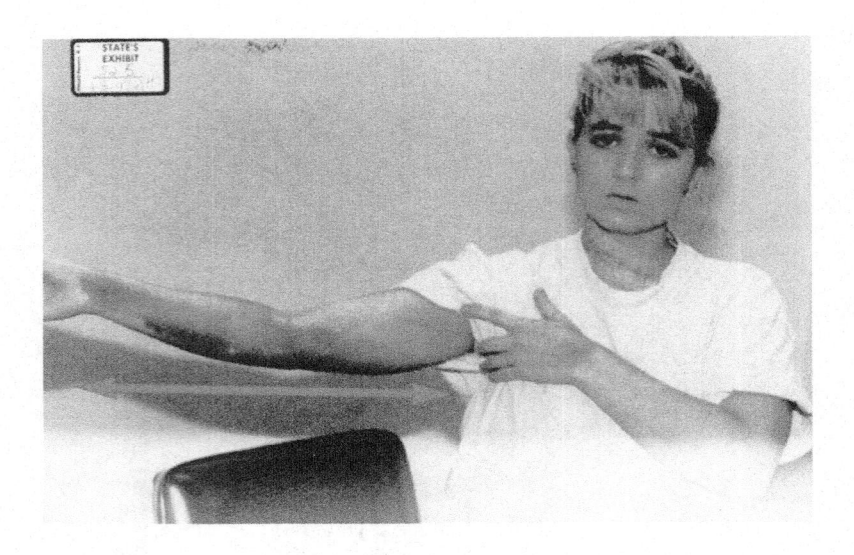

There is no bruising on the top portion of the arm so we can rule out that she was grabbed during the struggle that she claimed happen on the night of the murders.

Had these bruises been caused by someone grabbing and holding her arm tightly the bruising would be around the forearm and we do not see that.

And many people claim that these were caused by the attacker hitting her or her hitting him on that night.

If that were true then why don't we see any bruising at all on her opposite arm?

There is no way that anyone will convince me that she fought her attacker off to the extreme that she has major bruising to her arm and didn't use both of her arms to fight.

And at the same time if she fought her attacker with so much force and power to cause those injuries then why didn't she make any noise whatsoever while doing it?

I say this because Darin was only awakened when the wine glass broke and he heard Darlie scream.

It is hard to believe that she remained silent in a struggle that caused such bruising.

Most people believe that Darlie got those bruises by hitting her arm against the bed railing on her hospital bed.

They say this because the only major bruising is on the bottom portions of her arms. And that would be the only spot that she would be able to hit against the bed railing as she laid in the bed.

Also, there is less bruising to her left arm.

They believe that this is because it was her left arm that had the I.V. lines in, making it harder to slam against the bedrail without being noticed.

These next two photos are of her right arm.

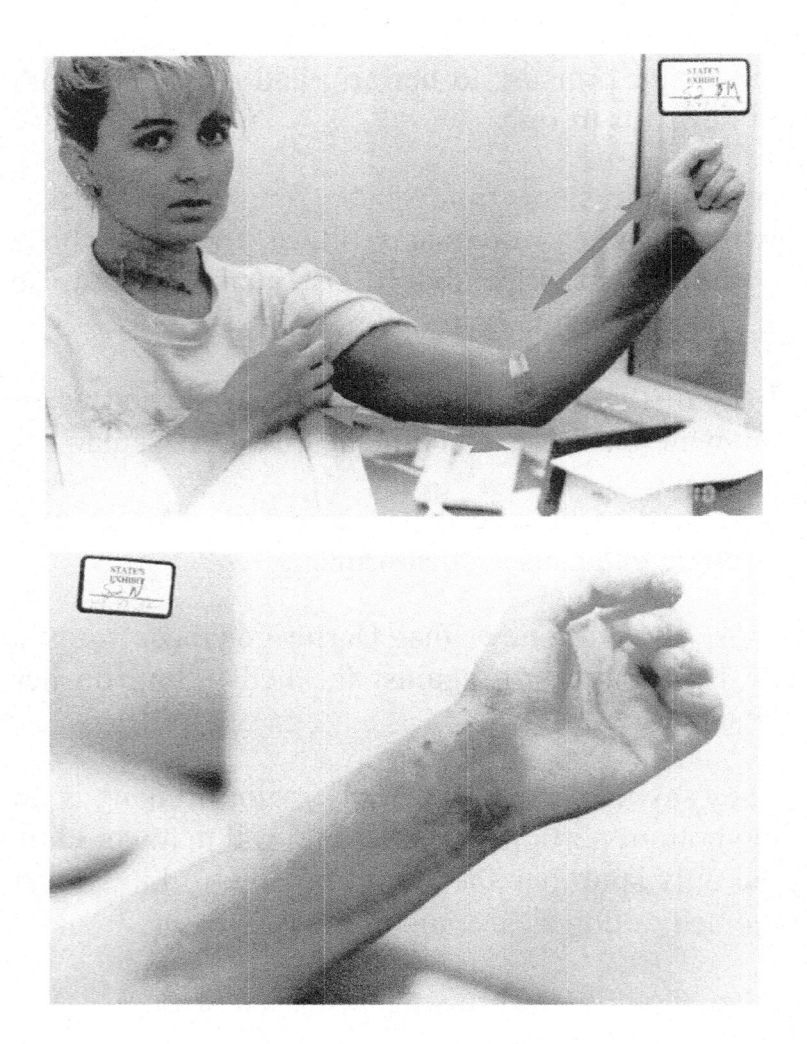

With the shape of the arm bruising in the bottom photo we can rule out that these bruises were caused by being grabbed as the bruising is straight and even. (Just like a bedrail)

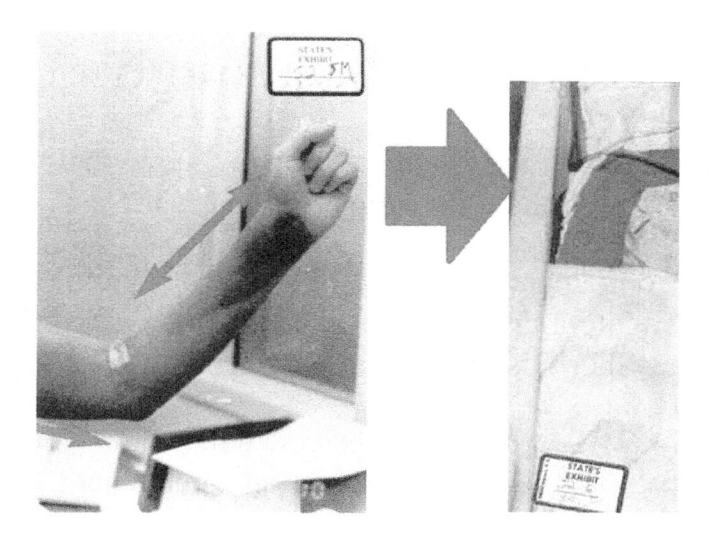

No matter how she was able to make these bruises we know for a fact that they did not happen from anything that she experienced on the morning of June 6th in her home.

Darlie was discharged from the hospital around noon on the 8th.

The funeral for the two boys was scheduled for later that day.

However, upon her release, she had to go to the Roulette police department first for questioning.

The Walkthrough

By 5:00 am the Roulette police knew that they needed more help investigating this crime.

The one person who they knew could help investigate a crime scene like this one was, retired Dallas Sheriff's Department officer James Cron.

Many of Darlie's supporters will want you to believe that James Cron was an uneducated hack who had no clue as to what he was doing.

What they leave out of their description of James Cron is that he was a commander in the crime scene search section and he worked for the sheriff's department for over 30 years.

He also holds certification as a senior crime scene analyst.

So I would guess that he does know a thing or two about investigating crime scenes like the one at the Routier's home.

Cron received a phone call from the Roulette Police department dispatch center around 5 am that morning.

The caller didn't relay much information to Cron, just that the crime scene officers asked if he would meet them on Eagle Drive because they had a homicide investigation that they would like his assistance with.

He arrived at the scene at about 5:45 a.m. and met with Sergeant Nabors, Officer Mayne, and Sergeant Matt Walling.

Cron asked them what type of situation they had. As he was only informed that it was a homicide and he asked them how many bodies they had, and did it occur inside or outside of the house.

After gathering the information from the officers at the scene, Cron made his way into the house with Sergeant Walling and David Mayne, about ten minutes after six, to visually inspecting the crime scene.

David Mayne was a crime scene technician whose job was to collect evidence, photograph the crime scene, and was also the manager over the evidence section of the Roulette Police Department.

Cron needed to walk through the crime scene to determine what equipment he would need. And to put together a game plan to collect and process the crime scene properly.

The men entered the house and went into the foyer leading into the hallway to go to the rear portion of the house.

Cron just looked at the floor, the walls, the ceiling, and the adjacent rooms to the left and right.

He was looking for blood or what appeared to be blood or evidence of a crime. There was blood in the entryway and hallway.

The men continued down the hallway to the family room and kitchen area.

Cron noticed several areas on the carpet that had excessive amounts of blood. There was a dead child in the back part of the room. And the coffee table was knocked ajar.

After seeing Devon's body lying in the living room Cron went into the kitchen area.

In the kitchen he observed some blood on the floor, more in the areas you step from the family room into the kitchen, there was blood on the floor.

He noticed some broken glass on the floor, and there was a vacuum cleaner lying on the floor.

There was a bloody knife laying on the edge of the counter.

To his right, there was a wine rack and to his left, he noticed that there were some open drawers, with some bloody cloth items on top of them.

As Cron continued through the kitchen, he noticed there were some drops of blood on the floor leading into the utility room.

In the utility room, he observed blood on the door and the floor, and there was a cap on the floor.

After looking over the utility room the men made their way into the garage.

Once inside the garage, Cron noticed a window partially rose with a cut screen.

He also noticed that the overhead door was closed.

But the one thing that he did not see was any evidence of blood on the garage floor.

Cron walked over to the overhead door and looked to see if he could see any bloody prints. He found none.

He also wanted to see if the door was latched or not because he was making a plan of what to go back and do later in the garage when he started putting together the details of the crime.

He also searched the floor for any type of evidence, like pieces of glass from the kitchen floor because there was broken glass on the kitchen floor. He found none.

He then went over to a window that was open looking for in that part of the garage for a trail, be it blood, glass, disturbance, that is areas disturbed to possibly follow the trail of an intruder.

And again he found none.

He looked at the window itself to look at it for evidence of blood and he found none.

He examined the windowsill and again found no evidence of blood. But what he did find was a fairly thick layer of dust over the entire windowsill.

He noticed some objects on the left-hand side of the window and some sort of animal cage on the right.

He looked on the floor for any signs of an intruder going through this open window.

He was looking for Disturbed dust, footprints, blood, any outside debris that might have been carried in through the window on the killer's clothing or shoes such as bark, mulch, any type of damp vegetation, just any signs that an entry and exit was made through the window.

And once again he found nothing.

The only thing out of the ordinary that he found was an undisturbed solid layer of dust along the entire length of the white windowsill.

After looking over the garage the men went around the side of the house towards the backyard.

Once outside the house, they searched the area for any signs of attempted points of entry at other windows, disturbed ground under the windows, cigarette butts, footprints, blood, and maybe a murder weapon.

And they found none of this outside of the house.

Once they arrived behind the house, they went up the driveway leading to the back gate.

On the driveway, he looked for signs of blood, skid marks, and possibly any objects that might aid his investigation, cigarette butts, and discarded weapons.

He searched the outside portion of the garage door for signs of pry marks, or for signs of attempted entry, and blood.

And he found nothing.

The men then examined the gate and then went inside the backyard.

Cron noticed the window that had the screen cut, and the partially opened window.

He searched the area outside of the open window for blood and any signs of an intruder.

And again he found nothing to support the theory that an intruder came in or left out of that window.

He then searched the backyard by the fence.

He was looking for signs of someone traveling through the mulch that was in the areas where an intruder might have left the window to the gate.

He also looked for scuff marks on the gate, to see if there were any signs of blood or scuff marks or any signs of a person possibly scaling the fence to get out of the backyard.

He then took special notice of the mulch area between the open window and the screen.

He knew that a person fleeing a violent crime scene would take the shortest route possible from the window to the gate and out of the backyard.

Especially knowing, that Darlie was following behind him and he needed to get away as fast as possible.

Cron looked in this area of mulch for signs of disturbance looking for any dampness or signs that feet were drug through the area, or fast movement of a heavy object, to see if it traveled through the mulch.

Cron even walked flat-footed, very gently or easily across the mulch and nothing happened.

Then he walked very fast across the mulch and was able to disturb it. He then ran across it and the dampness under the upper layer of mulch was then exposed and was darker than the top layer, and it became evident that he ran through it.

Then, he bent down and used his hand to ruffle up the mulch, and it appeared dark wherever he disturbed it.

After doing this test it was obvious to Cron that the intruder didn't run across the mulched area of the yard which seemed very strange to him.

So if the killer didn't run across the mulch then he had to of ran along the concrete walkway leading to the gate. This seemed very odd to Cron.

He searched the spa area and again found no sign of an intruder even being in there.

He also noticed that he could see the inside of the Routier's home through the Venetian blinds that were covering the sliding glass door.

So obviously the intruder had to know that the TV was on in the living room and that someone was home at the time.

They then went and checked the exterior of the fence for scuff marks and blood.

Again he found none.

At this time Cron was done with his initial walk-through of the crime scene.

The entire process took 25 to 30 minutes and due to lack of evidence he knew that an intruder had not entered the house through that open garage window.

Many people doubt this onion. But a man with around 39 years of experience would know what to look for in a crime scene to tell if the story that the victim is saying matches the physical evidence.

The entire scene indicated to him that there had not been an intruder.

And the physical evidence there at the crime scene was inconsistent with the information that he had been given by the Rowlett police officers before starting his walk-through.

The main thing that we have to look at is the point of entry and the point of escape. In this case, they are both the garage window according to Darlie.

"In the United States, modern standard bricks are (controlled by American Society for Testing and Materials i.e. ASTM) about 8" long × 3 ⅝ wide × 2 ¼ inches tall (203 × 92 × 57 mm). The more commonly used is the modular brick 7 ⅝ long × 3 ⅝ wide× 2 ¼ inches tall (194 × 92 × 57 mm). This modular brick of 7 ⅝ with a ⅜ mortar joint eases the calculation of the number of bricks in a given run."

So we know that a standard brick is 2 ¼ inches tall if you use a standard or a modular brick.

And if we add a ⅜" mortar joint between the bricks we have a total width of 2.625.

We will round this up to 2.75 inches per brick with the mortar included.

We see that the window in the garage is opened 9 bricks high.

And the cat cage is blocking the opening at the 9th brick from the wall to the right of the slit.

So the entire opening for a person to crawl through is only 24 ¾ inches by 24 ¾ inches.

Now many of Darlie's supporters still claim that a full-grown man, in a rush to flee a murder scene with a victim right behind him armed now with a knife, could climb through this window without disturbing the screen in any way. (The screen was not ripped and the only opening was where it was cut)

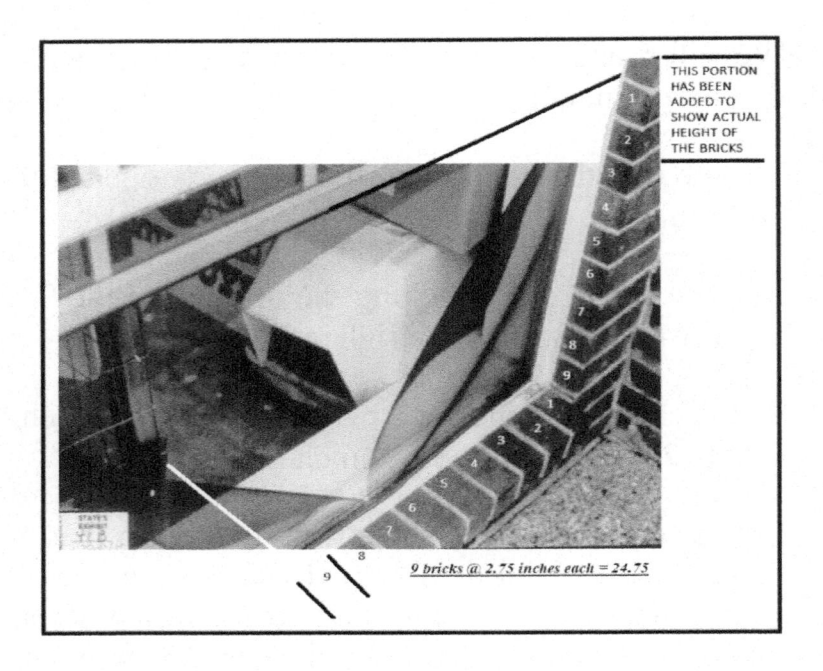

So by the diagram above, we know for a fact that the opening that the killer could have passed through is this size. And they would have left some trace amount of physical evidence behind.

The only physical evidence discovered at the window was one single strand of hair.

When the forensic testing was done on the single hair, it did come back to belonging to Officer Sarah Jones of the Rowlett Police Department.

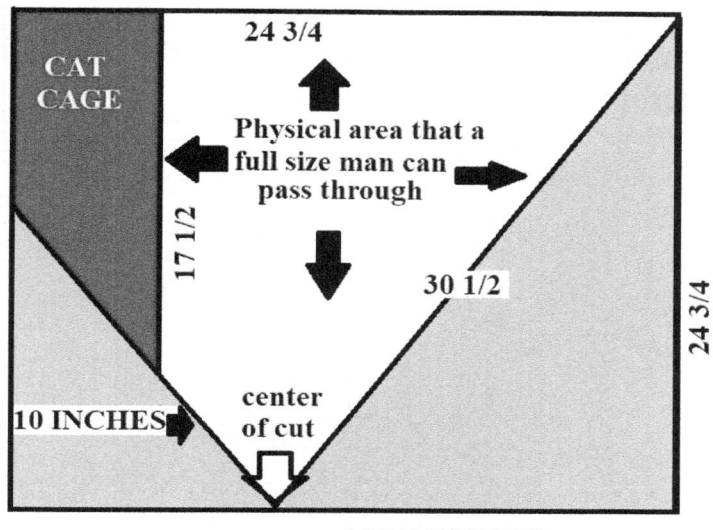

[Diagram: Cat cage area with measurements showing 24 3/4 (top), 17 1/2 (left side), 30 1/2, 24 3/4 (right side), 10 INCHES, center of cut, 17 3/4 INCHES (bottom). Arrows indicate "Physical area that a full size man can pass through."]

That diagram may not detail the area available for a full-size man to pass through in a frenzy to flee a murder scene.

I was able to recreate the actual opening based on the size in the police photo using a rope as a stencil.

I used a common item (Gas Grill Propane tank) to represent the width of the opening so that the reader can have something to compare to.

And when we overlap the diagram and the picture you can see the comparison.

I doubt that a full-size man would fit through the opening without ripping the screen further or disturbing the dust on the windowsill.

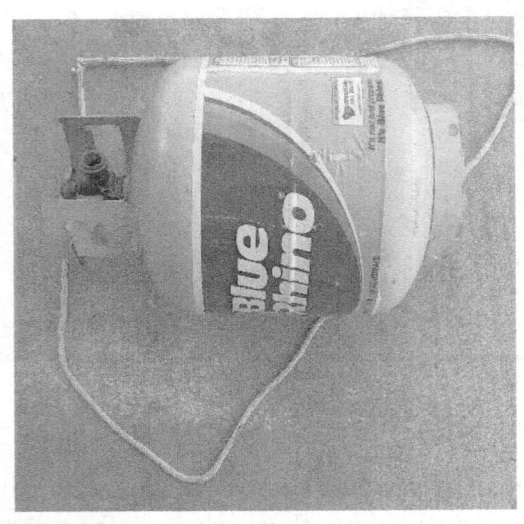

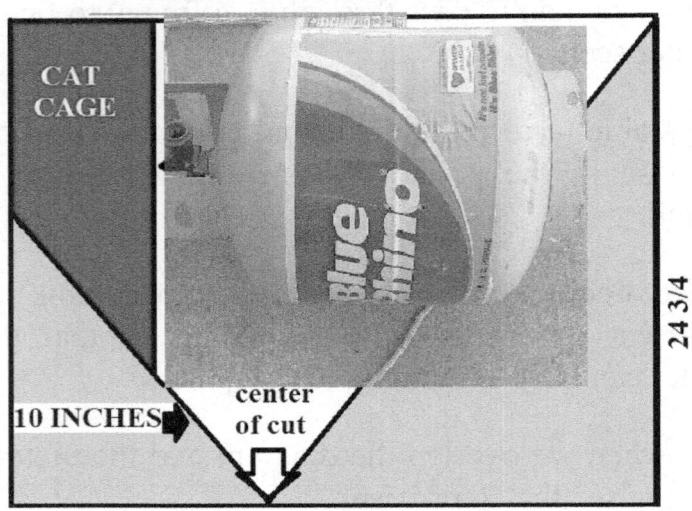

158

The police had possession of the Routier's home for the next 13 days while they collected evidence and DNA sample throughout the home.

I want to point out here that any boot prints found in the Routier's home were matched to the shoes or boots of the responding emergency personnel and police officers. There are no unknown boot prints in the house.

The Investigation Begins

Many of Darlie's supporters claim that they only accused Darlie of the murders because of the way she looked.

That the investigators didn't focus on any other person besides Darlie and that Darin was never even questioned.

If anyone believes that Darlie was singled out solely due to her appearance then they are wrong.

Cron never saw Darlie in person when he walked through the crime scene that morning, so he had no reason to frame her for the killings based solely on her looks.

And to believe that the police only looked at Darlie and never even suspected Darin is ridiculous.

Darin was questioned by the police.

If you are a Darlie supporter and you truly believe that Darlie is telling the truth in her statements 100% then you will see that Darin could not have committed the crime.

One of the reasons that Darin was ruled out was the fact that Darlie herself stated that her attacker went out through the garage and that she physically saw Darin come down the stairs from the second floor after she screamed.

It doesn't take a rocket scientist or much common sense to figure Darin's innocence in the eyes of the police investigators.

If Darlie states that Darin was not the attacker because by her account he was upstairs at the time, then what would make the police believe that he did it.

Others have claimed falsely that Darin may have drugged Darlie and caused her to be confused or disoriented on the morning of the attack.

Besides the fact that Darlie was very aware of what was happening around her when she talked to the 911 operator proves that she was not confused or disoriented.

When Darlie went to the hospital her blood was drawn and tested for drugs. And the only thing that was discovered was the diet medication that she was taking to lose weight.

All of this information can be found in her case reports.

Here are some of the other facts of the case that Cron and the other investigators found when processing the crime scene over the next two weeks.

And the physical evidence did not match up to the story that Darlie was trying to convince everybody that happened that night.

I also want to take this time to discuss the topic of items being moved in pictures that the police took of the crime scene; in particular the knife.

Many of Darlie's supporters fixate on the fact that one picture will show the knife on the counter while the next photo does not.

The reason for this is for the police to get a photo of what is underneath an item at a crime scene.

This is not a smoking gun of the police planting evidence; it is basic crime scene investigation techniques.

Let's start with the murder weapon itself.

The knife used in the killing came from the butcher block located on the counter in the Routier's kitchen.

This is one thing that made the police question the story that Darlie was giving regarding the events of that night.

If a person entered the house intending to rob it, then why were all of the valuables that were set out in the open for a robber to see not taken?

If the motive was to enter the house and kill the kids and Darlie then why did he not bring a weapon to do this?

Many of Darlie's supporters claim that the motive was just to rob the home.

But when one of the boys woke up and seen the robber he decided rather than fleeing the scene, he would kill everyone in the room.

Now we could say that maybe in some slim chance the situation did go that way. And the robber panicked and decided to kill any witnesses that could identify him. And that is why he chose to use the butcher knife that he found in the butcher's block.

The police sent the butcher's block and all of the knives to the Southwestern Institute of Forensic Science's trace evidence lab on June 8th for further examination.

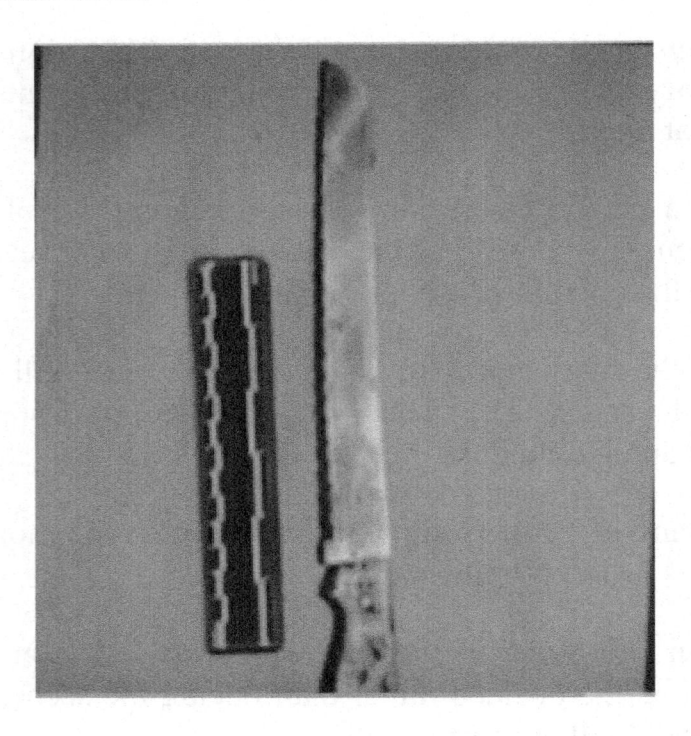

When the other knives in the butcher's block were inspected they found a bread knife that had a fiberglass rod on it that came from the screen that was cut in the garage.

Also, present on the bread knife was rubber debris with glass particles embedded and dark pigmentation.

Many of Darlie's supporters claim that the fiberglass rod did not come from the screen, but came from a fingerprint dusting brush used by Charles Hamilton of the Rowlett police department to dust the knives for prints.

And they claim that the rubber debris with the glass particles embedded and a dark pigmentation came from the dust used to detect fingerprints.

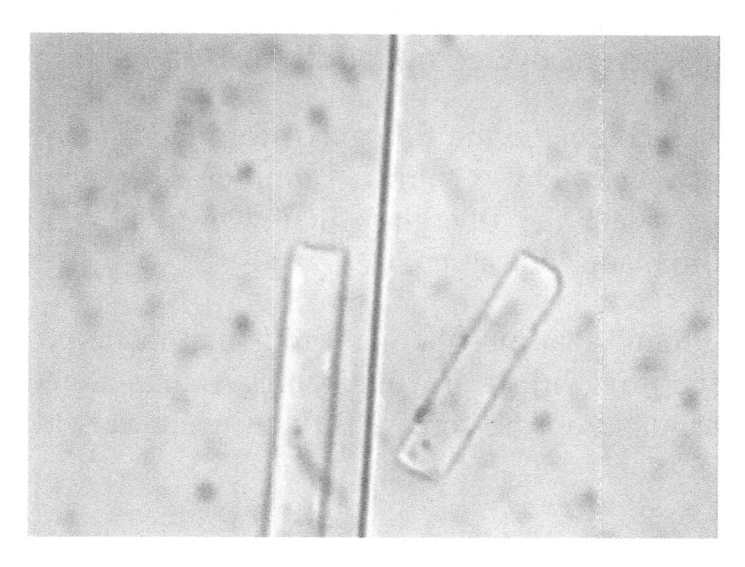

The fiberglass rod on the left came from the screen that was cut in the garage. The fiberglass rod on the right was found on the knife.

Charles Linch, the lab technician, conducted ten to fifteen test cuts on an identical screen from the Routier's garage.

Every time he ended up with fiberglass rods that were in every way microscopically identical to the one that he recovered from the bread knife.

He also ended up with the very same rubber debris with glass particles embedded and dark pigmentation.

This debris was also microscopically identical to the debris recovered from the bread knife.

Linch compared the fiberglass from the fingerprint brush used by Charles Hamilton's fingerprint brush with the fiberglass that was found on the knife blade and screen.

He found that the fiberglass rods that made up the fingerprint brush are much bigger than the rods that made up the screen. So they were very, very different.

So, for Darlie's statements to be true, the killer would have had to:

1. Break into the house in some other way than the cut window

2. Takes a knife from the butcher's block, and then goes back outside the same way he came in, cuts a screen on the garage window, and then he lets himself back in again.

3. Returns the first knife to the butcher's block and removes a second knife to kill the two boys and attack Darlie.

Darlie said the intruder threw the butcher knife down in the entrance to the utility room. She picked it up, and then walked back through the kitchen, placing the knife on the kitchen counter.

That knife blade was covered in blood on both sides when photographed by investigators.

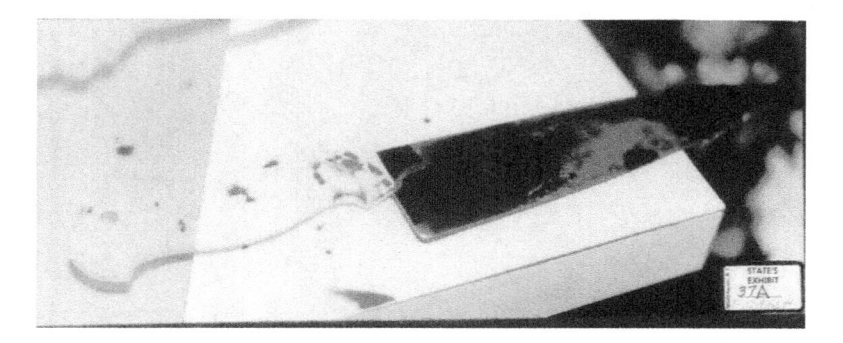

What the investigators found in the utility room were numerous round drops of low-velocity blood, belonging to Darlie, which indicated little or no movement when the blood was shed.

I will note that none of the websites that support Darlie's innocence will show a photo of the utility room floor where she claims the killer dropped the bloody knife as he fled into the garage.

I believe the reason for not sharing the photos of the utility room floor is because it disproves Darlie's claim that the killer dropped the bloody knife on the floor as he fled.

The police did tests to show how the blood from the knife would show up on the floor if it had been dropped as Darlie claimed.

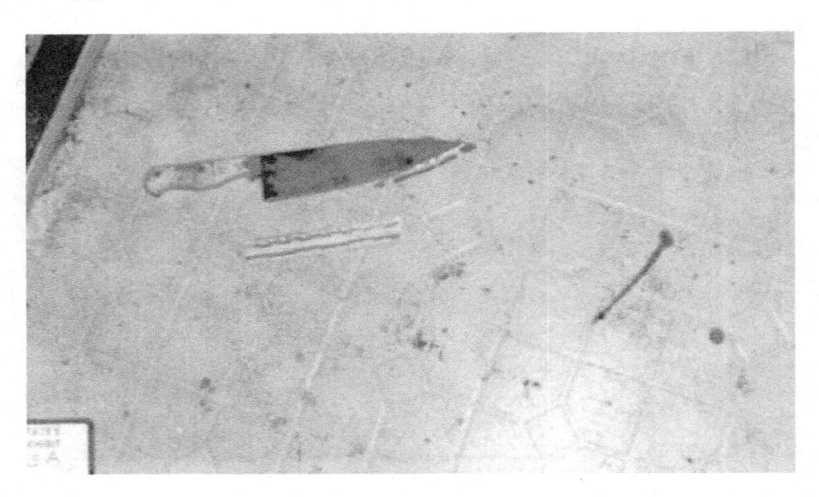

This is the actual police photo of the results of their testing of dropping the knife at approximately waist level while running/walking on the utility room floor.

And you can see that the blood left an obvious outline where it landed on the floor.

They even considered the possibility that the knife tip may have stuck in the floor rather than landing on its side.

However, after closely examining the floor they could find no evidence of the tip's impact on the linoleum.

They even considered the blood drops and the drops were slow-moving or low-velocity drops.

A slow-moving individual left those drops.

Many of Darlie's supporters have even claimed falsely that the picture used to show how the blood would be left on the utility room floor had the knife been dropped was an actual crime scene photo.

They claim that the blood on the floor left by the falling bloody knife is solid proof that the knife was dropped as it did leave an imprint on the floor as it should have.

But the truth is that there was never an imprint on the floor where a bloody knife fell to the floor.

And this is solid proof that the knife was never dropped as it did not leave an imprint on the floor as it should have.

When the police tested the blood that was on the knife, the only blood that was found was that of Darlie and Damon.

There was no blood on the knife from Devon. This means that the killer must have cleaned off the knife

Now if we are to believe Darlie's version of events that night, then we have to believe that the killer washed the knife off after stabbing Devon before he stabbed Damon and attacked Darlie.

I will also note that the only fingerprints discovered on the murder weapon were Darlie's.

Darlie was so worried that when she picked up the murder weapon that the killer's prints would be destroyed.

This was a very strange statement to say at that time regarding the situation that was going on around her.

Especially since Darlie would not know if her picking up the murder weapon would destroy any other prints on it. Or she was trying to explain why the police would not be able to detect anyone else's fingerprints on the knife besides Darlie's.

What Darlie did not know was that picking up the knife would not remove someone else's prints from the knife.

At the most, her prints would just be on top of the other prints and the police would see that.

However, they only found Darlie's prints just as she told them they would.

Darlie's blood drops in front of the wine rack and sink were also low-velocity drops, almost perfectly round, and consistent with a slow-moving individual leaving those blood drops.

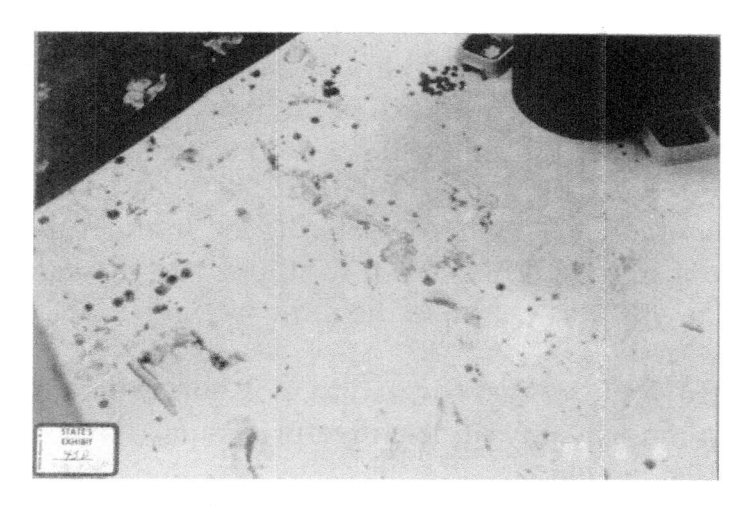

Not a woman running through the kitchen as she first stated.

And not the blood drops of a person running between the sink and her dying boys to bring towels to help save their lives.

In Darlie's statements to the police right after the murders she stated, "I got halfway through the kitchen and turned back around to *run* and turn on the light, I *ran* back towards the utility room…I *ran* back through the kitchen and realized the entire living area had blood all over everything."

And just like all of the rest of the evidence found by the police that goes against her storyline, by the time she had to testify at her trial, the "runs" in her story had changed to "walks".

This evidence completely contradicts Darlie's claim that an intruder dropped or threw the knife on the floor when he exited the house and that she ran between the sink and her dying sons.

You may be asking yourself, "If the intruder never dropped the knife or even went out into the garage then why was Darlie in the utility room?"

I truly believe that she had to make up that story to explain why any of her fingerprints may have been on the handle.

Darlie's blood on the floor, as well as on the washer, proves that she went into the utility room.

And from the blood pattern on the floor of the utility room, she didn't just grab the knife and run back out as she first claimed.

It should be noted that Darlie insisted she did not go into the utility room that night and that the knife was just a little bit into the doorway of the utility room.

During her trial, this is what Darlie said about what happened and where she was when she picked up the knife.

I got into the kitchen, and I got to where the island is, there is an island in the middle of the kitchen. I got to where the island was, and it was at that moment that I realized that I had blood on me. And I kept going, walking a little bit, and I saw a knife laying in the utility room.

The knife wasn't completely the whole way in the utility room; it was just like, a little bit into the doorway of the utility room.

It was an instinct -- I picked up the knife, it was an instinct to pick up the knife. I didn't think about it. It was just an instinct. I picked up the knife; I brought the knife back to the kitchen counter, and set it up on the kitchen counter.

At that time, I started to walk into the living room and it was at that time that I saw Devon, and he was laying on the floor, and he wasn't moving and his eyes were open, and he had cuts on him that were so big.

So in her trial testimony she never actually entered the utility room.

However, her blood on the utility room floor says that she is not telling the truth and that she did go into the utility room.

I believe that she went into the utility room to unlock the door leading into the garage so that the intruder could have a way into the house in her storyline.

Inside the utility room, the police found blood smeared on the door leading to the garage and blood drops on the side of the washing machine next to the door.

All of these were Darlie's blood.

[Photo of washing machine with arrows pointing to "DARLIE'S BLOOD"]

One thing that I need to point out in the above crime scene photo is the height of the blood and the amount of blood.

If we look at the blood running down the side of the washer we can tell that it is a very significant amount of blood.

Some of Darlie's supporters claim falsely that the blood got on the washer when the killer dropped the knife on the floor and it splattered up on the side of the washer.

I will say that if the knife had that much blood on it to send that much blood up onto the side of the washer, then why was there no blood on the floor where the knife was supposedly dropped at.

And we also know that the blood was dripped from above where the drop landed on the side of the washer.

This means that Darlie had been standing next to the washer and bleeding heavily to have her blood drop onto the side of it.

The police also found blood on the door itself belonging to Darlie.

But how could all of this blood be in the utility room if Darlie (by her own words) never entered the utility room?

Her supporters claim that the blood was left by the killer as he fled out into the garage.

If this was true, and the killer had so much blood on him that he was leaving actual drops of Darlie's blood behind as he fled the house, why did it end at the garage door?

If the killer had that much blood on him then we would find Darlie's blood in the garage and or on the window or gate that the killer was supposed to have fled through.

And what about the sock that was discovered down the alley behind the house?

If the killer had so much blood on him that he was dripping Darlie's blood at the crime scene then why was there no blood belonging to Darlie found on the sock?

The Darlie supporters cannot explain how he could have so much of Darlie's blood on his hand and none on the sock.

And if he had the sock on his hands to not leave any fingerprints then how did the blood smear get on the door with the partial fingerprint?

And what about the smeared fingerprint on the glass top table? How did he leave that in blood and get none on the sock?

And as for the rest of the blood on the table top, why isn't it blood that is running down the glass if it was tipped over?

In this picture, you can see the blood on the glass table top.

The biggest portion of blood in the center of the photo is a line of multiple blood drops. They were dropped onto the table as the person was moving and bleeding above the table.

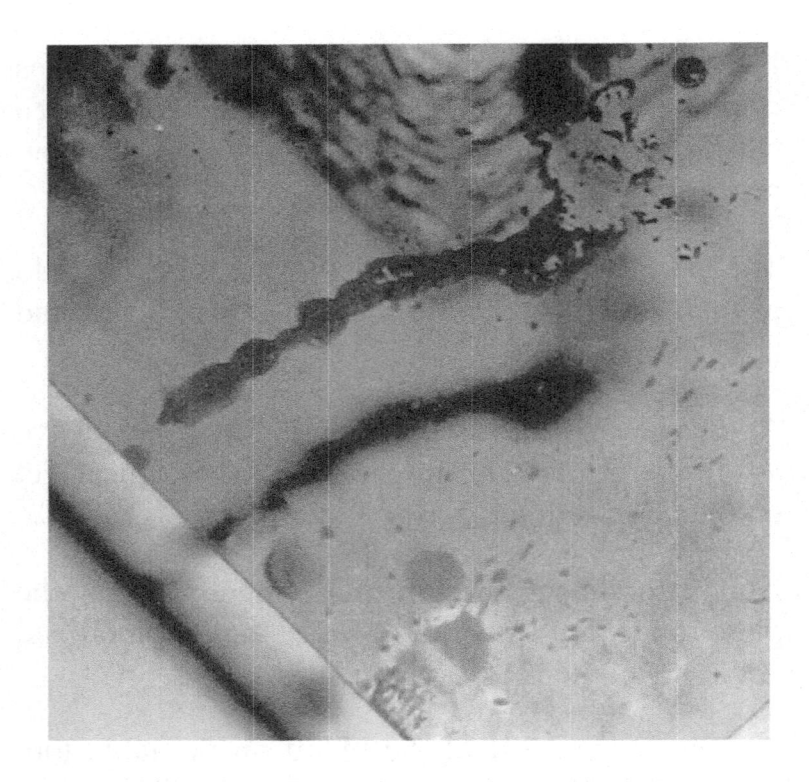

The blood drops on the bottom portion of the photo are also round which is caused by someone bleeding and the blood dropping straight down onto the glass.

If the glass table was tipped over in the struggle while Darlie was on the couch, then the blood would not be deposited in a straight-down fashion as we see here. It would have been cast-off blood with tails.

She would not have been standing over the table top and dripping blood from the couch.

And if the blood hit the table top while it was on its side the blood would be running down the glass.

The wine rack in the Routier's kitchen is another item that we need to look at.

A wine glass was broken and the glass was shattered across the floor between the wine rack and the bar in the middle of the Routier's kitchen.

Darlie told the police that the killer caused the wine glass to break and shatter as he fled from the crime scene.

After the police dusted the wine rack for fingerprints Cron shoved the wine rack, rattled it, bumped it, and jarred it to see if any of the wine glasses would fall off and none did.

The wine glasses would have to be lifted over a small lip which is like a U-shape at the end of the holders to be removed from the rack. This is a safety feature of the wine rack that prevents glasses from accidentally falling out.

An intruder hooking a single glass with his arm or elbow as he walked past would be next to impossible.

He couldn't dislodge any glasses without tilting it forward so far that they would all fall out of their rack.

This caused the police to doubt Darlie's story that the killer had knocked a wine glass off the rack as he fled because the wine rack was not knocked askew or pushed away from the wall.

If someone had bumped or run into it, it would have been pushed away from the wall.

Cron also found several small items, such as ice tongs and a bottle opener still balanced on top of other containers.

It was obvious that had the wine rack been hit hard enough to dislodge a wine glass then the smaller items would have fallen from their locations also.

So if someone hit the wine rack with enough force to cause the wine glass to come up over that holder or lip then why wasn't there enough force applied to dislodge some of the smaller items?

It was obvious that Darlie herself threw the wine glass on the floor to simulate a struggle with an intruder.

I will also add that if Darlie had been running towels from the kitchen sink to the family room to her sons, as she stated, then why didn't she have a single cut on either of her feet?

Darlie's supporters also claim her innocence based on three fingerprints taken from the Routier home

One of the prints was left in blood on the glass coffee table in the family room.

It is believed that this print would have come from a young child as e size of the grooves in the print are too small to be that of an adult.

However, one expert contends that one of Darlie's fingers cannot be identified or excluded as the source of the bloody print on the glass table.

The second print was a bloody print found on the utility room door.

The third print was a latent print that was identified and lifted below the bloody print on the utility room door.

Darlie has been excluded as a source of the prints on the utility room door.

After Cron completed his walkthrough he was convinced that an intruder did not enter the Routier's home and that Darlie's version of events did not match up to the physical evidence that he observed at the crime scene.

He questioned the entry and exit point through the cut screen in the garage. And the fact that there was no physical evidence to support a person passing through that window.

He questioned the motive behind the crime. If it was robbery why weren't any valuables stolen? Especially since they were left out on the counter in plain sight for a robber to spot?

He noted that the wounds on the two boys were very similar; that is deep, penetrating wounds.

However, Darlie's wounds were different in context, different styles of wounding.

Also, Darlie was cut on the neck and both sides of her shoulder and a deep wound to her forearm.

She claimed to have fought off her assailant.

There would have been some cast-off blood from Darlie flailing her arms to fight off her attacker.

However, he did not find any cast-off blood, on the glass tabletop, the walls, or any blood cast off that would be related to a struggle.

And if we are to believe that Darlie got her black and blue arm wounds from fighting off her attacker. Then her blood would be all over the area of her attack because she would have been bleeding from her arm and neck wounds.

He questioned the fact that Darlie said that her attacker did not say anything while he was attacking her.

This is very unusual.

When somebody is fighting with a live victim, especially when a fight is a man against a woman, vulgarity is commonly used, as well as a lot of threats.

He did not believe that the wine glass fell out of the wine rack as Darlie stated due to the amount of force needed to dislodge a glass. And the other items were not disturbed on the wine rack and it was still up against the wall and not moved from its original location.

This told Cron that the wine rack could not have been hit with enough force to make a wine glass fall to the floor.

And the fact that Darlie was supposed to have run through the glass on the floor to follow the attacker.

Go back and place the knife on the counter.

Transport the wet rags to the boys multiple times,

And yet, have no cuts from the broken glass that she walked through on the bottoms of her feet.

Also, the glass that was broken on the floor landed on top of Darlie's bloody footprints.

So the glass had to have been broken AFTER Darlie passed through the kitchen with blood on her feet and not before like she told the police.

And as far as bloody footprints go, there was no blood found beyond the utility room door that led out into the garage.

All of the blood from the crime was detained within the house. With as much blood that was found on Darlie's shirt and the floor of the living room, one would expect to find some blood outside of the utility room beyond the utility room door.

The star in this picture shows exactly where Damon was lying on the floor. You can see that there is blood all over the carpet area where he was lying.

And you can see that no bloody footprints are going around the vacuum that lies between the sink and where Damon is located.

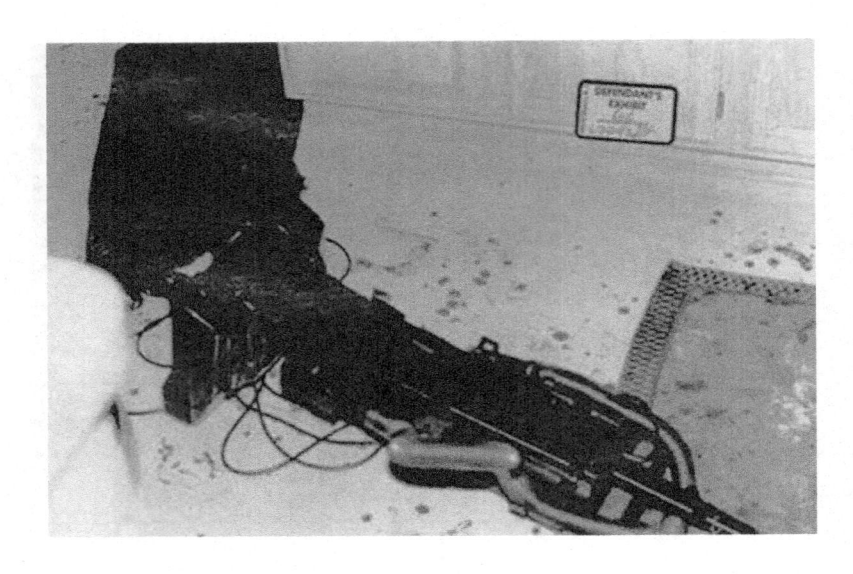

Here is the same area looking from where Damon was lying and looks toward the kitchen at the sink area.

In the second photo, you can see that no bloody footprints are going from the sink area which was covered with blood on the floor where Darlie was standing to where Damon was located.

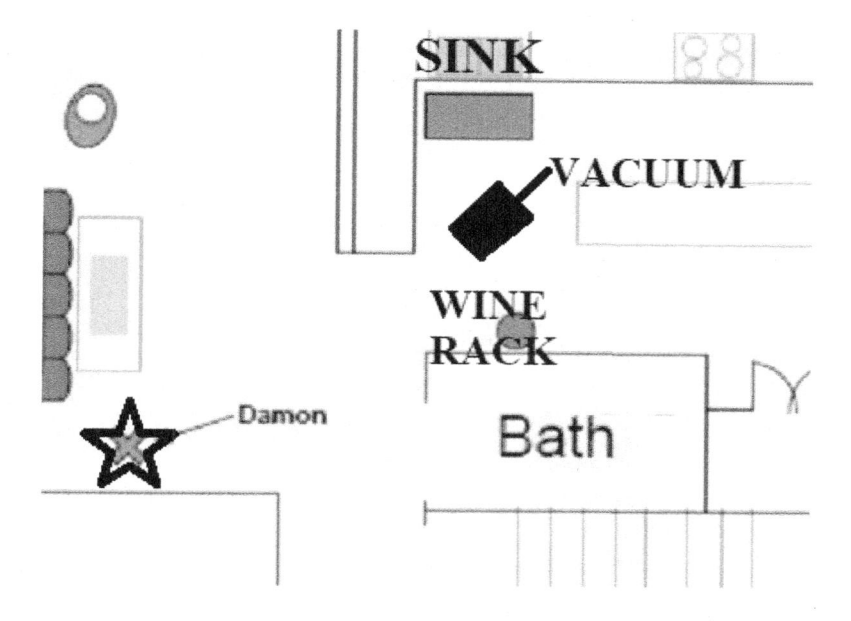

This diagram shows where Damon was located compared to the wine rack, vacuum, and sink.

Cron also had a problem believing that a killer would have committed a crime like this and gone to the great care of shutting a gate behind them and latching it. Even though the gate was difficult to open and close.

He also could not believe that a killer would drop his murder weapon and in this case, arm the person who is in pursuit of them.

And he discovered that the vacuum cleaner was on top of some of Darlie's bloody footprints.

Many of Darlie's supporters have focused a lot of energy on the vacuum cleaner and the blood underneath it.

So we will also take a closer look at the vacuum. We know 100% for sure, that the vacuum cleaner had been tipped over near the kitchen sink.

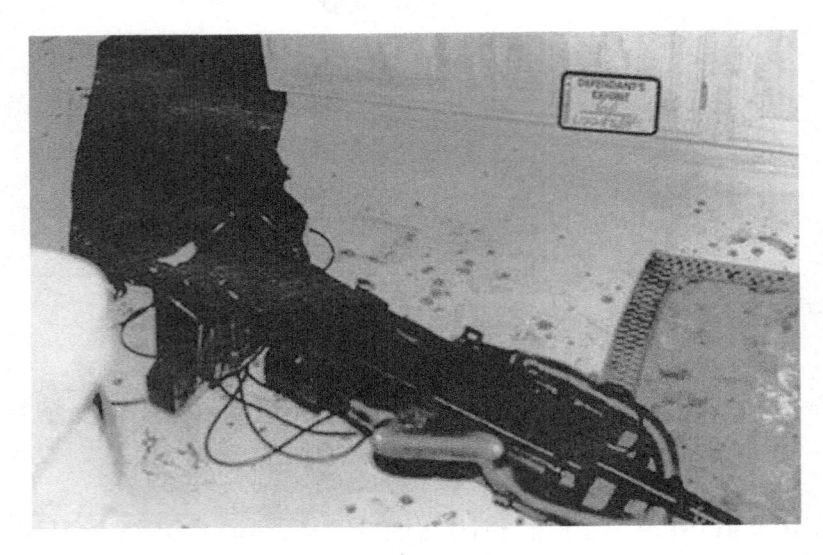

And we know that underneath were two bloody footprints leading away from the sink, toward the family room that came from Darlie.

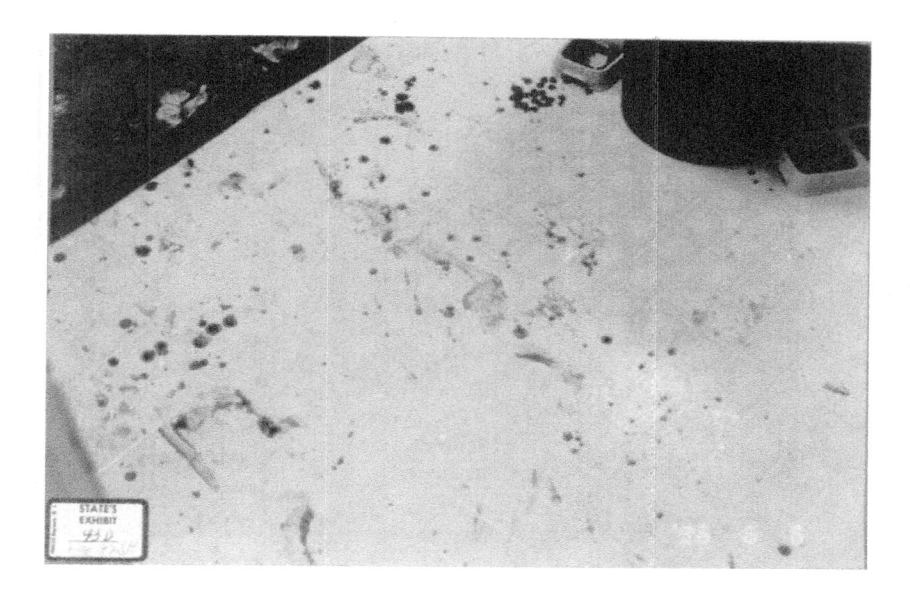

The police discovered that on top of those footprints were pieces of broken glass from the wine glass.

They also realized that there was no blood on the glass, which means that the glass was broken after Darlie left the bloody footprints.

When they took a closer look at the vacuum they saw where Darlie's blood had dripped down onto the top of the vacuum cleaner while it was standing upright.

Her blood was also discovered on the handle of the vacuum.

She made no mention of the vacuum in any of her initial statements to the police.

However, she had an explanation once she learned that the police were questioning the blood on the vacuum and the fact that bloody footprints were discovered beneath it.

She said that she'd been leaning over the vacuum for support and then "kind of took it with me" when she sat down.

Many people say that Darlie is lying as she never sat down where the vacuum was located in the kitchen.

However, when the police arrived Darlie was standing up. Officer David Waddell told Darlie to sit down because he saw the blood on her shirt and didn't know if it was coming from her or not.

He even testified that Darlie sat down and it was from her sitting down position that he questioned her. He also testified that she stood right back up.

So in my opinion, the vacuum could have been in that position if Darlie was leaning on it and it is lowered when she sat down.

And maybe the wheel marks in the blood could have been made by her moving the vacuum.

Some say that it was done to stage a struggle. But I doubt that because I believe that had she purposely put the vacuum in that position to create a storyline then she would have stated something that included the vacuum.

Over the two weeks following the attacks the police combed through the home looking for any evidence that could prove that a person entered the home and killed the two boys and attacked Darlie.

Many of Darlie's supporters will say that the police did not have experienced investigators investigating the crime scene. And that they did not do a thorough search for clues inside the house.

The two lead investigators in the home search were Charles Linch who was employed as a trace evidence analyst at the Institute of Forensic Sciences in Dallas and Kathryn Long who is a forensic serologist at the Institute of Forensic Science in Dallas.

So yes, they had two very qualified individuals investigating the crime scene.

The two investigators arrived at the house shortly after twelve o'clock noon on the day of the killings.

When they went to the area of the kitchen sink the front of the sink had a tremendous amount of blood on it. And the actual basin of the sink appeared to be clear.

On closer inspection, they noticed there were about seven stains that could visually be seen, that appeared to be dried but they appeared to be like washed out blood.

It looked as if someone had washed their hands or somehow the blood had mixed with water in the sink and had dried in little spots in the sink.

193

They also found blood on the left handle of the cabinet below the sink.

They found blood on the bottom of the handle. (*Not the top which could be caused by blood dripping down on it from above*)

It was somehow transferred to the bottom of the handle and would be consistent with an individual with blood on her hand reaching down and pulling that knob to open that cabinet door.

And inside of the cabinet, they found a streak of blood that would be consistent with the door having to have been opened when the blood was shed.

However, in none of her statements did Darlie say that she opened the cupboard door below the sink for any reason.

Darlie initially told the police that she never stood at the kitchen sink that night.

However, the same day that the investigators physically removed the kitchen sink to take it to the lab for testing, Darlie suddenly remembers that she was in front of the sink supposedly wetting towels to place on the boys.

The issue with Darlie's statement and the blood found at the sink was in Darlie's arrest warrant.

"Darlie has never mentioned to us being near the kitchen sink, which is on the west wall of the kitchen, during or after the offense. The physical evidence investigators examined that area and determined that there had been significant quantities of blood that was shed immediately in front of the sink. Although attempts had been made to clean the countertop and sink, tests with Luminol revealed blood on the top of the counter in front of the sink and on the floor.

The police also doubted her story about being cut while lying on the couch.

This was also stated in Darlie's arrest warrant.

Nabors, Cron, other officers, and I have all examined the couch where Darlie says she was sleeping when she was attacked; although there are quantities of blood throughout the room and around the boys, there was no appreciable blood on the couch where Darlie's head, neck, and shoulders were located at the time she says (in one of her versions) she was stabbed by her assailant. Our opinion from this blood evidence is that Darlie self-inflicted her wounds while standing at the kitchen sink."

When the investigators looked at the faucet on the sink, they were no visible blood on them.

When the investigators sprayed the basin and faucet of the sink with Luminol it showed that there had been blood present on these areas but had been cleaned.

Luminol is typically used at crime scenes where no blood is visible to the naked eye. It can detect hemoglobin, a key component of blood.

Luminol can detect the presence of blood even if it has been diluted hundreds of thousands of times.

The Luminol also proved to the police that not only was blood rinsed down the sink; it was also wiped up from the counter on the sides of the sink.

Now many of Darlie's supports will claim that the blood was washed away when she was running back and forth to wet towels to apply to her dying sons.

This was also proven by the physical evidence to not be true. No water or diluted blood was found on the kitchen floor.

At no time did Darlie run from the sink into the living room multiple times to bring wet towels to her boys.

We know this for a fact as no bloody footprints are leading to and from the sink to where the boys were lying on the floor.

And the fact that Devon's body was covered in blood (not diluted blood) told the investigators that a wet towel was not used on him as it would have removed the blood from his chest.

No towel was found on Damon's back and no indication that a towel was ever used on him.

Here are photos of the floor at the end of the bar in the kitchen. Darlie would have had to go through this area to get from the sink to the living room area where her boys were located. And you will see that there are no bloody footprints or any disturbed blood droppings in this area to support this claim.

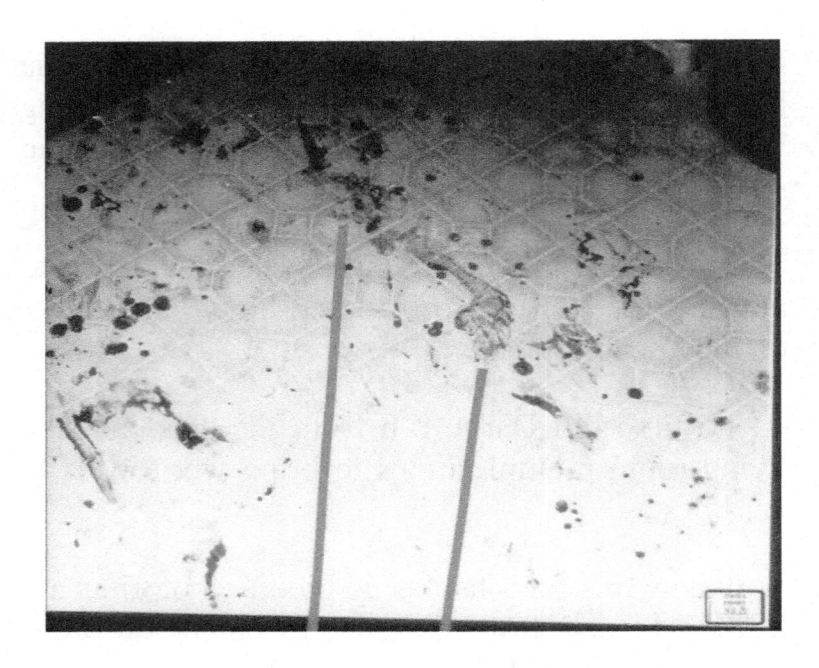

This photo shows where Darlie passed through the area one time that morning.

If she had been traveling through this area as much as Darin and she claims, there would be more bloody footprints and the blood drops would be disturbed.

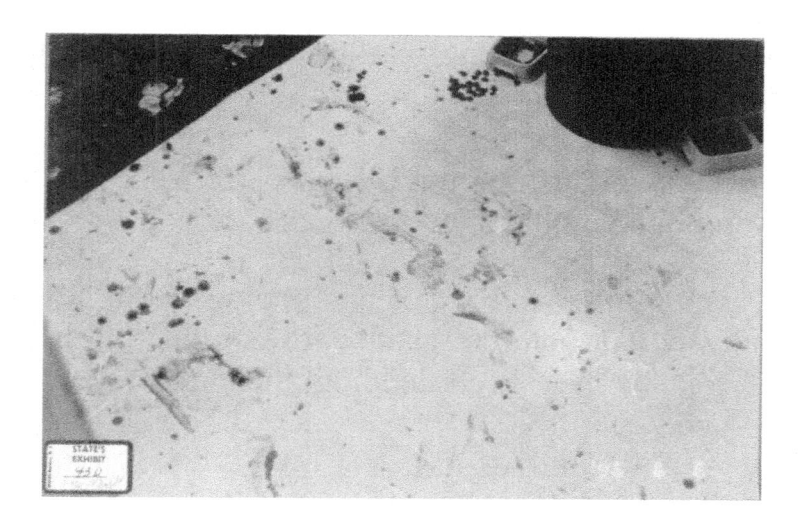

Many of Darlie's supporters claim that she had to have been bringing towels to the boys because the police found towels all over the place.

Again, this is a false statement made by Darlie's supporters to push their narrative that Darlie is innocent.

The police removed a total of 21 towels and washcloths from the house.

3 damp towels were taken from the utility room

2 towels from the laundry basket in the utility room

4 washcloths were taken from the top of the stairs

3 towels were taken from the backyard spa

None of these twelve were connected to the murders.

The remaining nine towels taken from the house were found within the crime scene area.

2 hand towels were found and photographed in the hallway, but both only had Darlie's blood on them where she had been holding them to her neck wound.

1 towel was found next to Devon's body.

Darlie's supporters claim that this proves that she was bringing towels to the boys. What they fail to state is that the only blood on the towel was Darlie's, and no water was found on the towel.

Most of the remainder of the towels were scattered around a good distance from the boys.

1 towel and 1 washcloth were discovered to have blood on them which were both identified as belonging to Darlie.

1 green and white washcloth in the kitchen area is the one Officer Waddell observed Darlie holding to her neck when he first entered the house.

Neither Devon nor Damon's blood was found on any of the towels collected from the crime scene.

The remainder of the towels came from the drawer in the kitchen.

They also tested the backyard gate and the latch on the gate, and they found no traces of blood.

They also tested the window that Darlie claimed was the entrance and exit point for the attacker and no traces of human blood was discovered.

The police even had the living room carpet removed from the home so that it could be searched inch by inch for clues.

What Charles Linch did discover was a bloody impression of the knife approximately 18" from Devon's body, where the bloody knife was set down on the carpet.

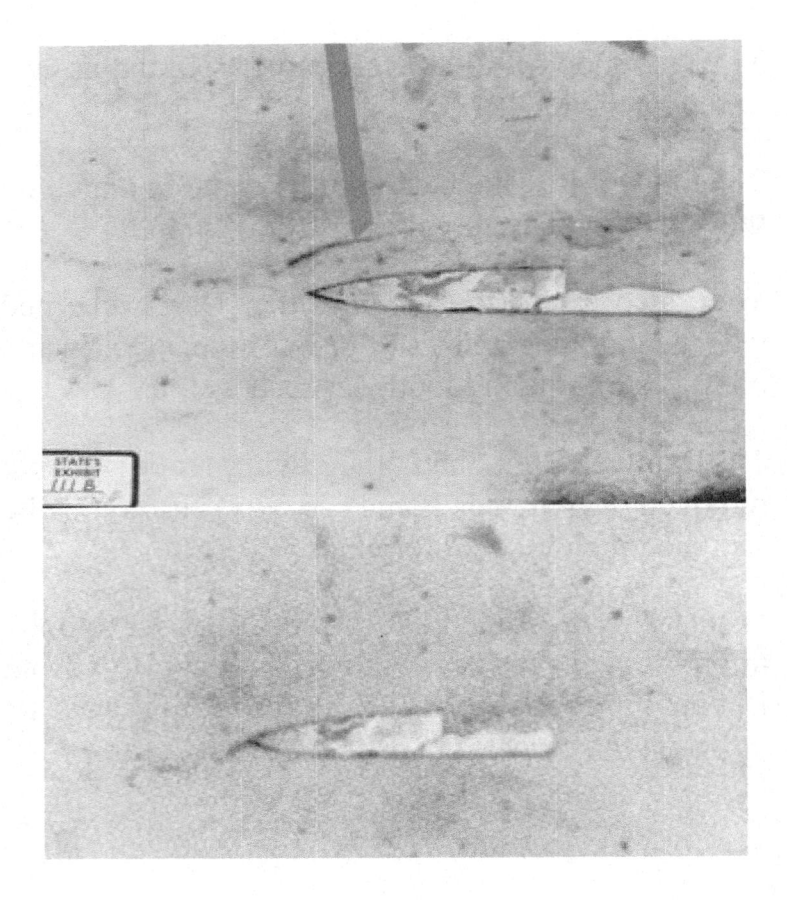

When we look closely we see a one-inch-long tail of blood from where the tip of the knife would have set on the carpet.

During the trial, this one-inch trail of blood was asked about and the explanation as to why it's there was that the knife has to be held above the area, to where the blood is dripping, and there has to be some backward motion.

This blood trail was not made by just simply laying the knife down on the carpet.

The one thing that all of Darlie's supporters refuse to address is that this blood outline contains Darlie's blood!

This means that the knife would have to of been laid down there AFTER Darlie was cut and bled on the knife.

-OR-

Considering that Darlie had a cut on her right arm that was bleeding and that the knife outline in the carpet was in Darlie's blood, then enough blood could have been running down the knife to cause it to drip off the end of the blade shortly before it was laid (not thrown or dropped) on the carpet.

When the investigation was completed it was obvious that an intruder did not come into the Routier's home and attack Darlie and kill the two boys.

The police tested the nightshirt that Darlie was wearing on the night of the attack.

And what they found also did not line up with the statement of events that Darlie was saying.

The stars located in the photos show the location of the boy's blood on Darlie's nightshirt.

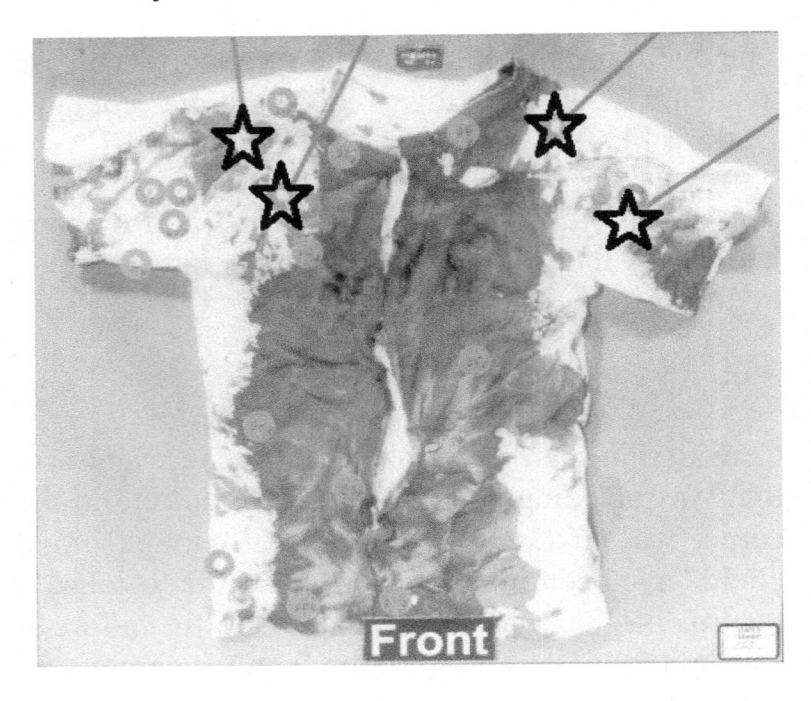

I want to point out that there was no blood from the boys located on the front bottom portion of Darlie's nightshirt.

Had she been applying wet towels to her son's wounds and if she was leaning over either one of her boys she would have blood on the bottom front where the nightshirt would have come in contact with the boy's blood. Especially with Devon who according to both Darin and Darlie had blood spewing from his chest wound when Darin tried to give him CPR.

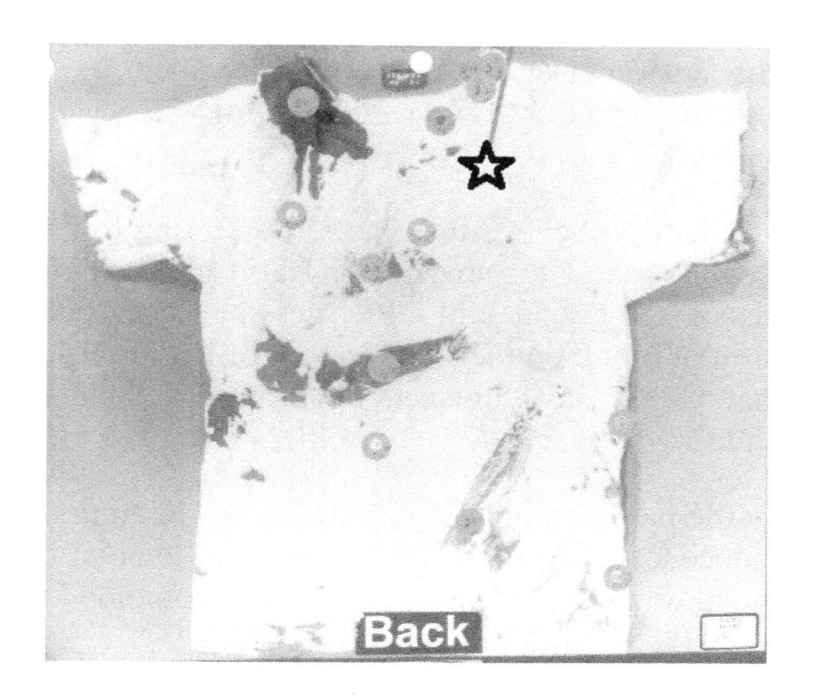

Darin's testimony at trial was that he tried to give Devon CPR: *"I put my hand over his nose, and I blew into his mouth, and when I did, this blood just splattered all over my face and was blowing air right through him."*

He was asked, *"Where was she when you were blowing into his mouth?"*

Darin stated that Darlie was, *"Right over the top of him."*

He was then asked, *"What was she doing?"*

His answer was, *"She was trying to stop the bleeding. She was trying to hold his chest together."*

It is hard to believe that Darlie was trying to hold Devon's chest together while Darin blew air into his mouth giving him CPR, yet she never got a drop of blood on the front bottom of her nightshirt that would have brushed up against the bloody child.

Darlie has even gone to the extent of claiming her innocence by pointing out the fact that some of the blood was a mixture of hers and the boy's blood.

This is a total smoke and mirrors technique as her blood could have easily mixed with the boys when she cut herself or as she held the towels to her neck injury.

The blood that was found on the front of the shirt was a mixture of Darlie and both of the boy's blood.

Many of Darlie's supporters claim that the blood was mixed due to the blood soaking together while it was being transferred to the lab for testing. This theory was disproven by DNA experts.

Because cast-off or spatter blood dries quickly because it has little volume.

The boys would have been stabbed at least 45 minutes to an hour before the nightshirt being placed into an evidence bag at the hospital. Considering the time between the blood being deposited on her nightshirt and her arrival at the hospital, all of the cast-off blood spots would be coagulated and dry.

The bloodstains found on Darlie's nightshirt were most likely the result of spatter or cast-off from when the boys were being stabbed.

These bloodstains had a long up and down axis, meaning the movement of the blood was from down to up.

Both stains were on the left shoulder area of Darlie's nightshirt and were the result of spatter or cast-off.

They also found a small blood spot that contained only Devon's blood and was most likely cast-off due to its location on the back right shoulder of Darlie's nightshirt.

Its long axis going in an up and down trajectory was consistent with Darlie raising the knife, depositing Devon's blood on the back of her shirt, then bringing her arm down to stab him again.

Darlie's lawyers argued that Devon's blood got on her nightshirt while Darlie was leaning over Devon as Darin performed CPR on his son.

However, Darin himself, before he changed his story, said that Darlie was in the kitchen while he was performing CPR on Devon.

It wasn't until her trial when he changed his story to say that Darlie was leaning over Devon trying to hold his chest closed while he performed CPR on his son.

And this statement only furthers the fact that they are not telling the truth. Darlie would have had more blood on her than just cast-off bloodstains on her shoulder area.

Darin stated that Darlie was in the kitchen on the phone to 911 at the time he performed CPR on Devon.

And we know by the physical evidence found on the kitchen floor (lack of bloody footprints) that Darlie did not travel from the sink to Devon multiple times to provide wet towels or to assist in the CPR.

So it would be physically impossible for any of the blood drops to travel from where the boy's bodies laid in the living room to where Darlie was standing by the sink in the kitchen.

But let's take a look at Darlie's statement to the police.

She said that she was lying on her back and seen the man leaving the living room area walking into the kitchen.

If she were lying on her back, as she claimed, the blood would not have been able to get onto the back of her nightshirt because she would have been lying on her back.

And, if she'd been lying on her side, the direction of the cast-off blood would be in the opposite direction than what it was.

The blood splatter would have been sideways instead of lengthwise.

And speaking of blood splatter, the one thing that NONE of the Darlie supporters, or any of the websites that claim her innocence talk about, is the fact that Damon was stabbed in two separate locations that night.

Damon's blood was located next to and on the couch where Darlie claimed to have been sleeping.

So this tells us that he was stabbed in that area first.

Damon's blood trail proves that he traveled from the couch area where he was first stabbed to the area by the hallway where he was found.

Darlie's blood was found in blood splatter on the wall near where he was found when the paramedics arrived.

The blood splatter indicates that he was stabbed in that location again by someone bleeding. (The DNA tests show the blood was Darlie's).

They avoid this fact because it does not line up with any of the multiple stories that Darlie said to the police.

Darlie places Damon right behind her as the killer flees the house through the kitchen. Her story does not explain how Damon was stabbed near the hallway where he was found.

When the police finished investigating the crime scene they knew that there was no intruder in the Routier's home that night. And seeing that Darlie's version of events did not match the physical evidence they knew that she was lying.

When the police discovered the Routier's financial situation, they believed Darlie may have wanted to get rid of her children because they were an expense that would prevent her from continuing to live her luxurious lifestyle.

And her mental state could have contributed to her committing the murders.

While many of Darlie's supporters claim that these are weak motives at best, these motives, combined with Darlie's statements and the crime scene evidence, were enough to make Darlie the prime suspect in the murder of her sons.

Mary Rickells, who lived two blocks away from the Routiers testified that she was watching television around 1:30 a.m. when she heard banging on her door.

She thought at first that it was her husband returning from work.

However, she became suspicious when she heard the sound of wood splitting and loud cracking noise.

She said that she turned on her porch light and saw two men, one had on a jogging suit, with long sleeves, and the other one had on a cowboy hat and a western-style shirt.

Neither of whom fitted the description of Darlie Routier's 'intruder'.

The men then ran from the house.

What is strange is, even though the wood of her door had been split, and she was alone with her 15-year-old daughter, she did not call the police.

Instead, she decided to return to finish watching a horror movie television.

But it gets even stranger.

A little later the same night, the men returned and tried to break into her daughter's bedroom through a window.

She testified that she just turned on the light and they ran off.

And again, even though she was home alone with her 15-year-old daughter, she chose not to call the police.

Even though she described her daughter and herself as petrified from the experience.

Many of Darlie's supporters claim that these were the same men who broke into the Routier's house and attacked Darlie and killed the two boys.

Besides the fact that neither of the men fits the description of Darlie's attacker, the timeline does not fit.

During the trial, Mary Rickells gave the time that the men were at her home.

Question, "Okay. So about what time was that?"

Answer, "Little after 2:00, 2:08, or somewhere around in there."

Question, "So, sometime after 2:00?"

Answer, "Yes, sir."

The men would not have had enough time to drive from the Rickells' house over to the Routier's and break in and commit the crime.

The mysterious black car that the Darlie supporters keep mentioning was not parked in front of the Routier's house as they claim.

Mary Rickels said that it was parked across the street from her house.

And that it was still parked out there at 7:30 a.m. on the morning of the murders.

And you can see from this map that the two houses are not even in the same neighborhood.

Numerous other leads were followed up by the Rowlett police department.

Darlie supporters claim that these sightings prove that Darlie didn't kill her sons.

What they fail to acknowledge is that all of the leads have been investigated and the physical evidence verses Darlie's statements say that she did kill her sons.

Arrest & Trial

Darlie was discharged from the hospital around noon on the 8th of June.

The funeral for Damon and Devon was scheduled for later that same day.

However, upon Darlie's release, she had to go to the Roulette police department for a second interview with Detective Patterson causing Darlie to arrive late to the funeral.

The following day, Devon and Damon are buried, hand-in-hand in a single casket in Rest Haven Memorial Park.

The decision to bury the boys holding hands would later cause a problem in the investigation.

Neither of the boys was fingerprinted before their burial.

And later in the investigation, their casket was dug up so their fingerprints could be obtained.

However, water had seeped into the coffin and degraded the fingerprints on the boys.

The following day after the burial, Detective Patterson once again interviews Darlie at the Rowlett police station.

It is at this interview that Darlie's wounds on her arms are noticeable.

Photographs of her injuries to her arms are also taken at that time.

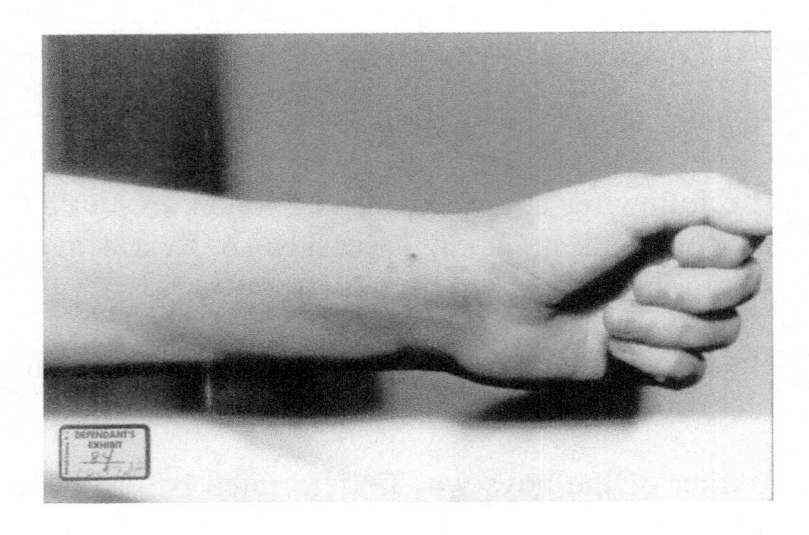

216

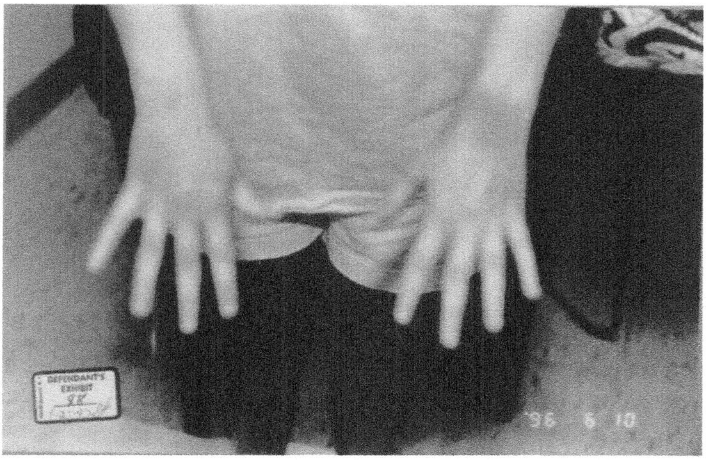
DEFENDANT'S
EXHIBIT
'96 6 10

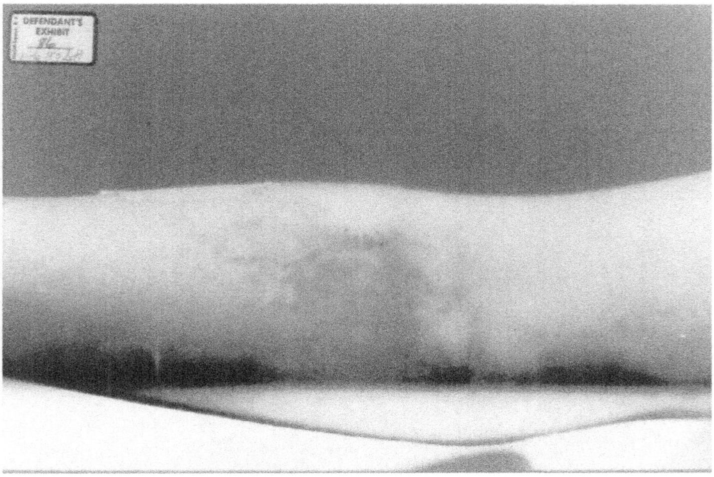
DEFENDANT'S
EXHIBIT

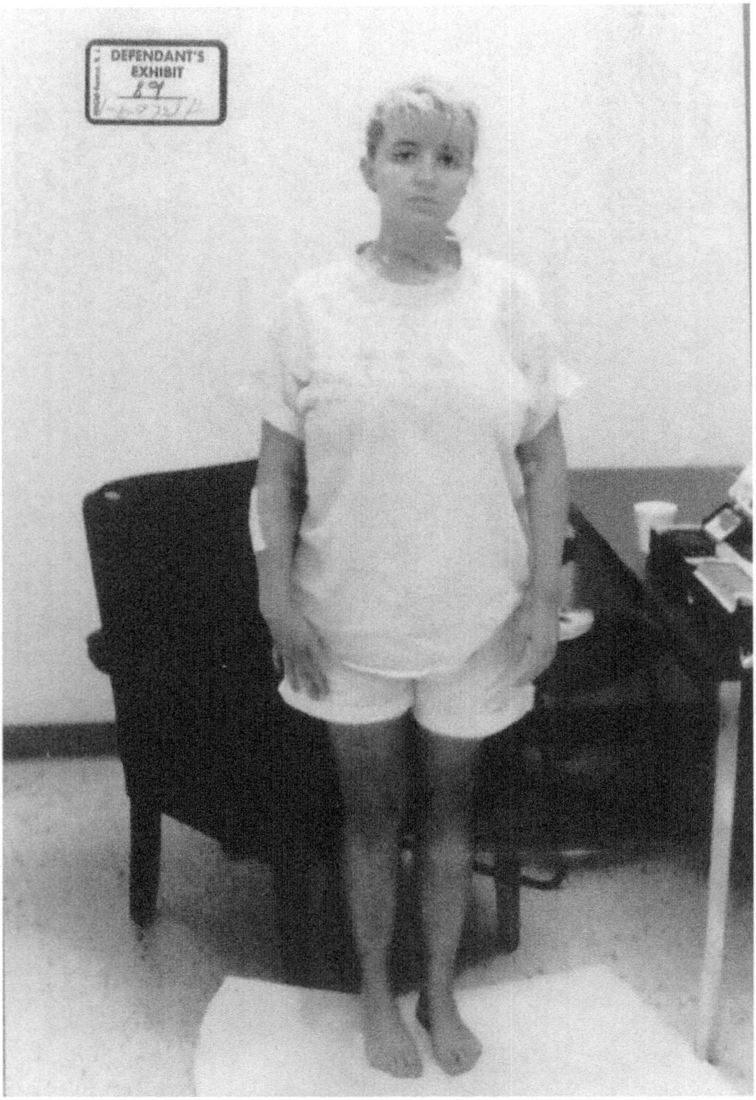
DEFENDANT'S
EXHIBIT
89

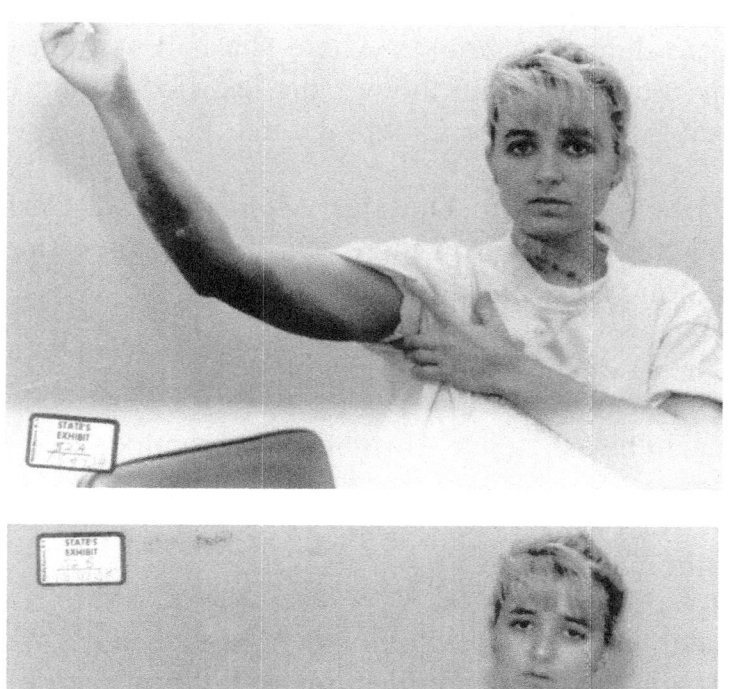

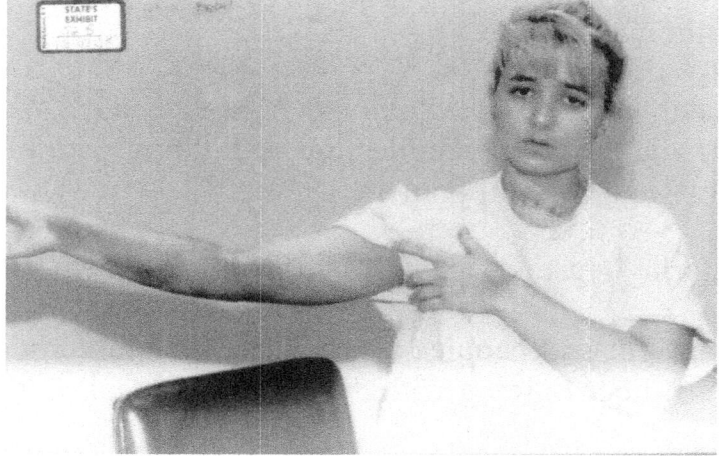

Interestingly, out of all of the cuts and bruises that Darlie had, the two areas she was the proudest of, her face and her breasts were mysteriously uninjured.

Darlie and her supporters claim that her bruises, all predominately on the underside of her right arm were defensive bruises where she had to fight off the intruder. (Even though she testified during her trial that she never fraught the man)

Darlie's attorney Douglas Mulder asked Darlie, "There is a word in there, Darlie, that they say is fighting and you said.

Darlie's response was, "Frightened."

Again he asked her, "Frightened? It sounds like."

Darlie's response again was, "I didn't say fighting."

Later in her trial testimony, he asked her, "Well, do you have any recollection of fighting with him, or struggling with him?"

Darlie's response again was, "No."

Now many people claim that she just didn't remember fighting with the man who attacked her.

That is also proven to be false because the physical evidence at the crime scene and Darlie's wounds don't support that theory.

There were no slashes or stabs wounds underneath her right arm where she was using it for defense?

Those types of bruises don't just come from someone grabbing your arm; they came from striking something very hard against it.

And the fact that Darlie fought with the killer on the couch to the point that she was cut on her neck and arm, received bruises from multiple blunt force hits, but never screamed for Darin causes me to question if a struggle happened.

And we also need to ask, why weren't her fingers or the palms of her hands cut while fighting a large man with a knife?

There is only a small scratch on two of her fingers that are not explainable by a fight with a man armed with a knife.

Some people believe that the bruises came from when the boys were kicking with their legs to ward off the stabs. (Especially the right arm holding the knife)

The trauma surgeon, an emergency room nurse, and four ICU nurses testified during the trial that the bruises under Darlie's right arm were not there while she was in the hospital and up to when she was discharged.

What is very interesting is that the prosecutor asked Dr. Santos how long it would take for bruising like this to occur to the arm after receiving this blunt force trauma.

Dr. Santos answered that it would take 24 to 48 hours.

Even Darlie's neighbor Karen Neal, who is also a nurse, testified that Darlie did not see any bruising when she went to visit Darlie in the hospital.

Darlie's supporters claim that a doctor and four nurses from Baylor University Medical Center lied about the bruises to help convict Darlie.

I highly doubt that they would risk their careers and risk receiving jail time by committing perjury on the witness stand to prosecute someone that they don't even know.

And for this to be true they would have been in on the scheme from the very first hour that she entered the hospital for them all to falsify her medical reports.

One thing that we need to acknowledge is the fact that these wounds did not appear until after she left the hospital.

And they were photographed by the police on the 10th of June.

EXACTLY 48 HOURS AFTER SHE WAS RELEASED FROM THE HOSPITAL.

The 48-hour timeframe is important because during the trial Dr. Santos was asked how long it would take for bruising like this to occur to the arm after receiving this blunt force trauma.

And his answer was 24 to 48 hours.

And when these photos were taken Darlie was released from the hospital for 48 hours.

I believe that if she did not inflict these wounds using the bed rail then she had the opportunity to do it once she was released from the hospital and before the police photos.

It's interesting how no one saw these bruises on Darlie's arm before June 10th, except for Darlie's family members.

Just 8 days after the murders, a video would surface that some say sealed Darlie's fate.

Police maintained video and audio surveillance of Damon and Devon's gravesite, **without a court order,** in the hopes of hearing Darlie break down or confess during a private, somber moment of remorse.

On what would have been Devon's 7th birthday, June 14, Darlie organized a posthumous graveside birthday party, where Darlie and her sister was videotaped spraying silly string over the balloons and flowers at the gravesite.

She laughed chewed bubble gum and sang Happy Birthday.

A local television station was invited along to record the event.

Darlie said, "If you knew my sons, you'd know they're up in heaven having the biggest birthday party we could ever imagine. And though our hearts are breaking, they wouldn't want us to be unhappy. But they'll be a part of us always. And they played with Silly String all the time."

This video was shown to the jury during her trial and many believe that this video is what ultimately convicted her.

I have watched this video numerous times myself online.

And I will say that Darlie should only be convicted by what happened in the house, not at the gravesite.

I say this because a second video that showed the somber tear-filled memorial that the family held was not shown to the jury.

Many of Darlie's supporters claim that the second video was withheld from the trial.

The prosecutor, Greg Davis turned the videos over to the defense before the trial began. And they refused to show the somber memorial video to the jury.

There is also some confusion around the fact that the Detectives involved in the video and audio surveillance of Damon and Devon's gravesite plead the 5th amendment and did not answer questions.

Darlie's supporters claim that this was a tactic not to answer questions that would have lead to Darlie being found not guilty.

And like most of their statements regarding this case, this was also untrue.

During the trial, Darlie's lawyer Doug Mulder called Detective Jim Patterson to the stand.

Detectives Patterson and Frosch had been the ones who authorized the placement of the surveillance equipment in the cemetery.

Mulder accused Patterson of committing a federal felony and told the detective he was going to jail.

Patterson told Mulder that if he was saying that he violated some state or federal law, then he was not going to answer until he had legal counsel.

Mulder replied that they better get legal counsel then because he was suggesting to them that that is exactly what they did.

So all Patterson and Frosch did was following Mulder's advice and retained attorneys who advised them to invoke their Fifth Amendment privilege against self-incrimination.

The trial judge, Mark Stenson *Tolle, ruled* that the detectives could not be questioned about the tapes. The prosecutor, Greg Davis told the judge that, although the defense had not entered the tapes into evidence, he had no objection if they wanted to show them to the jury.

He told the judge that whatever was recorded out there, he certainly doesn't have a problem with them doing that.

And so it was Darlie's defense that made sure that the jury has never seen any of the police surveillance tapes.

So it was Darlie's defense council that sabotaged the second surveillance coming into the trial.

Many people believe that her defense never showed the tapes because they did not show a grieving Darlie, as supporters have claimed over the years.

Darlie's mother, Darlie Kee and Darin sued the city of Rowlett, Patterson, and Frosch, and the assistant district attorney for invasion of privacy and search and seizure violations.

However, on May 28, 2001, the 5th Circuit Court of Appeals ruled against them, stating that there is no expectation of privacy in a publicly accessible cemetery.

On June 18th, just four days after the graveside birthday party, Darlie is told to come to the Rowlett police station for a fourth voluntary interview.

She is told midway through the interview that the police already have a warrant for her arrest; Darlie continues to talk to the detectives for another hour before asking for an attorney.

She is then arrested and charged with capital murder.

Darlie was booked into the Rowlett City Jail and arraigned by Municipal Court Judge Owen Lokken.

Judge Lokken ordered Darlie to be held without bail. Mrs. Routier was then transferred to the Lew Sterrett Justice Center.

On June 26th, Darlie was given a bond amount of $500,000.00 for each murder charge that she was facing, for a total of 1 million dollars.

On June 28, Darlie was officially indicted by a Dallas County grand jury of capital murder for the murder of Damon.

This was done because Damon was under the age of six at the time of his death and that made it a capital murder case.

Also, it was a strategic move by the state's attorney's office because if Darlie was found not guilty for Damon's murder they could always charge her later for the murder of Devon.

To protect the integrity of the trial, Judge Mark Tolle, who presided at Darlie's trial, issued a gag order on the same day as her indictment.

He barred the defense, the prosecution, potential witnesses, and even Darlie's immediate family from discussing the case with the media.

Which Darin, and Darlie's mother, Darlie Kee, violated the very next day by doing a live interview on a local radio station.

After Darlie's indictment, a bail hearing was held on July 5th.

Her defense attorneys requested that she receive a bail at one hundred thousand dollars or less.

The request was denied and she was ordered held on a 1 million dollar bail.

Also during this hearing, it was discovered that the Routier's youngest son Drake was now living with Sarilda Routier, Darin's mother.

Darlie was ordered to stay away from Drake if she was able to be bailed out of jail.

On July 10th, twelve days after being indicted, Darlie felt that she could not get a fair trial in Dallas County.

Due to overwhelming media coverage of the case her defense attorney filed a motion to have the trial moved.

Many of Darlie's supporters claim that it was the prosecutor's office who wanted the trial moved.

But in reality, it was Darlie's defense team who filed the motion with the court to have the trial moved.

Her trial was supposed to take place in Dallas, but it was moved to Kerrville, Texas.

Darlie received a major blow to her case while she awaited word from the judge on having her trial moved out of Dallas County.

On August 8, Greg Davis from the Prosecutor's office filed a motion to hold Darlie without bail.

His reason for this motion was the fact that they were now seeking the death penalty in this case.

On August 28, the judge agreed with Davis and ordered Darlie to be held without bond.

On September 12, Judge Tolle grants Darlie's defense motion for change of venue, moving her trial over 300 miles south of Dallas to Kerrville in Kerr County.

On October 16, 1996 jury selection process began in Kerrville, Texas.

On November 14, jury selection is completed and would consist of seven women and five men. In total, 165 potential jurors were interviewed by the defense and prosecution.

The trial was now set to begin at 9:00 a.m. on January 6, 1997.

On Friday, October 4, Darlie took a lie detector test.

The questions and results were never made public by her defense attorneys.

I will say that defense attorneys never hesitate to release polygraph test results when they come back as inconclusive or confirms that their client is telling the truth.

Seeing this was not the case we can only assume that the results were not in Darlie's favor.

Right after the test was done, Darlie's mother was asked about the test that Darlie took, and she did not have any knowledge of it.

The trial started on the 6th, with Greg Davis, the Prosecutor, reading the indictment against Darlie.

Greg Davis, "True bill of Indictment. In the name and by the authority of the State of Texas, the Grand Jury of Dallas County, State of Texas, duly organized at the January Term A. D. 1996 of the 194th Judicial District Court of Dallas County, in said court, at said Term; do present that one Darlie Lynn Routier...." Is that your true name?

Darlie, "Yes, it is."

Greg Davis, "The Defendant, on or about the 6th day of June, A. D., 1996, in the County of Dallas, and said State did unlawfully, then and there, intentionally and knowingly cause the death of

Damon Christian Routier, an individual, hereinafter called the deceased, by stabbing said Damon Christian Routier with a knife, and the deceased was, at the time of the offense under 6 years of age. Against the peace and dignity of the State. Signed, John Vance, Criminal District Attorney of Dallas County, Texas. Ray W. Paul, Senior, Foreman of the Grand Jury."

The judge asked Darlie's attorney, Mr. Mulder, "How does your client plead?"

Darlie replied, "Not guilty."

The judge replied, "All right, thank you, ma'am."

And the trial began with the swearing-in of the jury and the witnesses, followed by the prosecution and defense's opening statements.

The prosecution opened their case by offering the state's theory of the murder of Damon.

According to the state, Darlie was a selfish woman whose extravagant lifestyle was being threatened by the responsibilities of being a mother.

The prosecution said that if her two boys were dead, Darlie could collect on their life insurance and resume her wild ways.

The District Attorney argued that Darlie, suffering from postpartum depression, slit her own throat, and then tried to make it look like an intruder had attacked her and committed the murder.

During the trial, a medical examiner testified that Darlie's wounds were superficial and most likely self-inflicted. But the defense introduced medical records showing that the knife slash to Darlie's neck came within 1/16 of an inch of severing her carotid artery.

This was not helpful at all for Darlie's defense. As that did not prove that Darlie didn't cut her neck and just come very close to her carotid artery.

Darlie's attorneys questioned the theory that she committed the murders to collect on her boys' $5,000 life insurance policy.

Darlie's attorney said that if money was the motive, why wouldn't she kill her husband Darin who was insured for $800,000?

The prosecution also played a videotape for the jury of the Routier family celebrating Devon's seventh birthday posthumously. This video has come to be known as "The Silly String Video"

During the trial, Darlie insisted on taking the stand and testifying.

Darlie was her own worst enemy under cross-examination. The prosecution even commented later that Darlie was *their* best witness.

When the prosecution would point out inconsistencies in her statements and get her cornered, she would either start to cry and use what prosecutor Toby Shook referred to as "selective amnesia" and say "*I just don't remember.*"

She said that phrase over 70 times during her testimony

Darlie said that she could not remember the intruder's face. She could only describe to the police his clothes and the approximate height, but she stated that she either didn't look at his face or couldn't remember it.

Then while in jail awaiting trial in the first week of November, she wrote five letters to family and friends including one to her neighbor and friend Karen Neal, and her Aunt Sandy.

In both letters, Darlie stated "*I know who did it, Glenn did, I saw him. I know he did it.*"

In the letter to her Aunt Sandy Darlie stated: "*We believe we know who did it. That FBI guy is working on it. We have two months to work on it. We already have so much on him. I really believe he did it. Darin will have to tell you about him it's a long story, I know it's him. I saw him and I know it's him"*

The workers in the jail's mailroom intercepted the letters and gave them to the DA's office.

When prosecutor Toby Shook began reading the letters while Darlie was on the witness stand, she asked him: "Where did you get those? Those are my private letters."

Shook told her that the mailroom employees at the jail intercepted the letters and gave them to his office.

The courtroom spectators (including some jurors) started laughing when Darlie asked the judge if it was legal to do that.

Darlie knew that she was cornered and once again she began crying.

Shook produced the third letter and read a portion of it out loud. *"I know who did it, and it's driving me crazy that he is out there running free.."*

Then he read out loud the fourth letter to one of Darlie's friends stating, *"I'm praying they'll be able to get a confession from Glenn."*

Then he read a portion of another letter to her aunt, *"We know who did this and we're trying to get more on him."*

At this point, Darlie was crying non-stop and Toby Shook stopped reading the letters.

The man that she was referring to was Glenn Mize, who was a friend of one of Darin's employees.

Darlie had told Mize's wife about him swearing at their secretary and that she didn't appreciate it. In turn, Mize was upset with Darlie and supposedly called and threatened her according to Darlie.

Prosecutor Toby Shook brought Glenn Mize into the courtroom in front of the jury while Darlie was on the witness stand.

Glenn Mize didn't at all fit the physical description Darlie had given to the police of the intruder.

When he was presented to Darlie, she denied that he was the man that attacked her.

This was a major blow to her credibility.

She repeatedly told everyone at first that she did not know the attacker and that she has never seen his face.

Then she was adamant that it was Glenn Mize. Yet she couldn't remember that it was him right after the attack.

And then, when she is confronted with the fact that Glenn Mize does not fit the physical description that she gave of her attacker, she had to admit that she was wrong.

After 24 days of trial, closing arguments were on January 31st after which the jury was sent out to deliberate Darlie's fate.

During deliberations, the jury watched the silly string video eight times. It took them just ten hours to find Darlie guilty of the offense of capital murder as charged in the indictment.

On February 4, 1997, the jury recommended the death sentence and the judge agreed and sentenced Darlie to death.

Darlie Lynn Routier, the jury, having found you guilty of the offense of capital murder, and having returned an affirmative finding on the first Special Issue submitted to them at the punishment stage of this trial, and a negative finding on the issue of mitigation, it is now the duty of this Court to assess your punishment at death.

Is there any lawful reason why sentence should not be pronounced at this time?

There being none, it is the Order, Judgment, and Decree of the Court in this cause, styled the State of Texas versus Darlie Lynn Routier, Dallas County Number F-96-39973-MJ, and Kerr County Cause Number A-96-253.

That you shall be taken by the Sheriff of Kerr County, Texas, and shall immediately thereafter be delivered to the director of the Institutional Division of the Texas Department of Criminal Justice, or other person legally authorized to receive such prisoners, and shall be confined in said Institutional Division, in accordance with the laws governing the said Institutional Division, until such day, to be determined by this Court, and some time after the hour of 6:00 P.M., in a room arranged for the purpose of execution, the said director, acting by and through the executioner designated by the said director, as provided by law, is commanded, ordered and directed, by this Court to carry out this sentence of death by the intravenous injection of a substance or substances in a lethal quantity sufficient to cause your death until you are dead.

You are hereby remanded to jail until the Sheriff can obey the directions of this sentence.

You may be seated, please.

Darlie Routier was then taken the following day to death row at Gatesville State Prison's Mountain View Unit where she is awaiting execution as inmate # 999220.

As of March 2021, Darlie is one of only six women on death row in Texas.

There has been a false rumor going around the internet that Darlie was given an offer of life in prison during her trial.

And others claim that this offer was given to her during her appeal process to avoid going back to trial.

We know for a fact that she was not given a "life without parole" offer during the trial for one reason; Life without parole was not a legal sentence at the time that Darlie was awaiting trial.

It was eight years after Darlie's sentence that Texas Governor Rick Perry, on June 17, 2005, signed into law legislation that allows Texas juries to sentence defendants to life without the possibility of parole in capital cases.

Before this bill being signed, defendants in capital crimes were not allowed by law to get an offer of life without the possibility of parole.

Senate Bill 60, better known as death by incarceration. The law took effect on September 1, 2005.

So, there was no way that the offer was given to Darlie at the time of her trial.

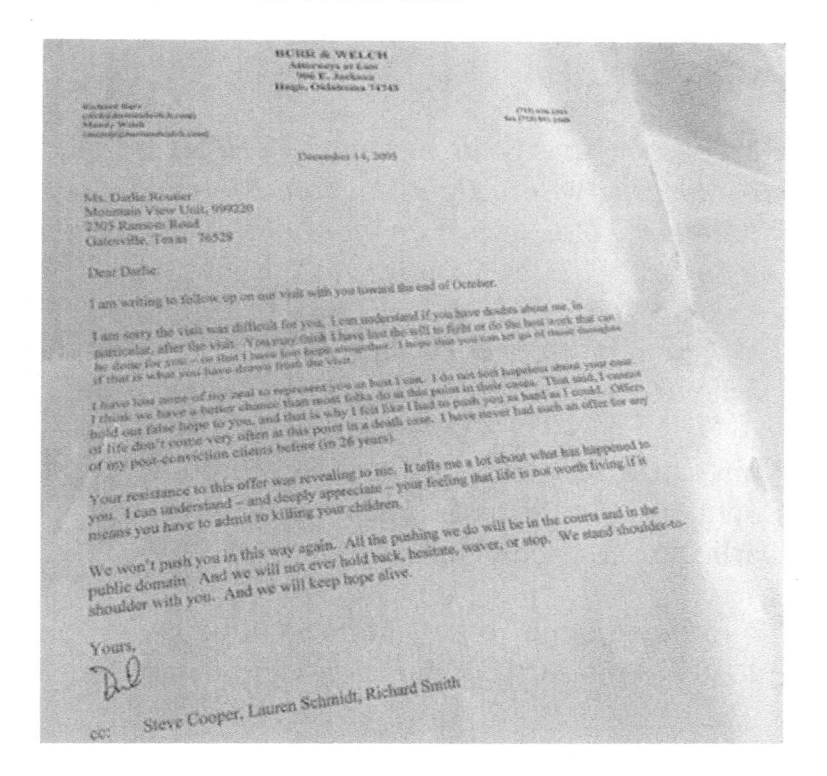

The letter that her supporters are talking about is dated December 14, 2005. Three months after the law went into effect.

I truly believe that Darlie may have told her attorney during a visit that she would not accept a plea deal of life in prison if it was offered to her during the appeal process to avoid another trial.

This would fully explain the excerpt from the letter that states: *Offers of life don't come very often at this point in a death case. I have never had such an offer for any of my post-conviction clients before (in 26 years).*

He goes on to say in his letter, *You may think I have lost the will to fight...or that I have lost hope altogether...that said, I cannot hold out false hope to you.*

This sounds like even he doesn't believe that Darlie had a good chance at winning a new trial.

You can also go online and search for, "Dallas County public records" and view every one of Darlie's case documents.

You can search case numbers F9639972 and F9639973 to see all of the case documents.

And in those documents, you will not find an offer document given to Darlie for life in prison without parole.

When Darlie's supporters are faced with this information they claim that the offer was only given verbally and not officially.

This is ridiculous as all plea offers are documented on a "Case Information Sheet"

Here is a case information Sheet from Darlie's case to show that an offer for a plea is part of a document used on her court proceedings.

And we can all agree that if Darlie was given a plea deal, her family would be waving it for everyone to see.

Fifteen months after Darlie was convicted, a Waco, Texas multi-millionaire, Brian Pardo, believed Darlie was innocent.

He spent $100,000 of his own money financing a private investigation of her case.

Pardo talked Darin into taking a polygraph examination to rule him out as a suspect.

Darin Routier taking a polygraph test

Darin denied the involvement of any kind and the lie detector determined that he was lying.

All he said was that the examination results were wrong.

Pardo dropped his financial assistance after seeing the overwhelming evidence against Darlie, and Darin's failing of the polygraph.

Darin later did admit to partaking in an insurance scam involving the Jaguar and that he had talked to people about staging a robbery for insurance purposes.

He said that he never carried through on it.

He said that he "talked to people" regarding robbing his house. Then why didn't he say this during the trial?

If my wife was attacked and my children killed by someone who they believe was breaking into my home to commit a robbery, then I would say that I spoke to someone about robbing my house.

He also admitted that Darlie had asked him for a divorce on the night of the murders. This was confirmed by Darlie's attorney, Stephan Cooper.

Many believe that this is what caused Darlie to snap and kill her boys.

Many, if not all of Darlie's supporters, say that the police didn't investigate Darin enough for the murders of the two boys and Darlie's attack.

At the very beginning, everyone was a potential suspect.

But as for Darin, Darlie herself had never told anyone, including the police, that he had been the assailant.

Pretty early on in this investigation, he was eliminated as a serious suspect.

The 2015 DNA results confirm that there is not one shred of evidence to show that an intruder came into the Routier's house or that the only other person in the house, Darin, was responsible for murdering his sons.

The physical evidence found at the scene of the crime, and the fact that Darlie's statements do not match the physical evidence, point to no one else but Darlie.

It did in 1996 and still does today.

It was later discovered that the trial transcripts contained numerous errors.

Those errors have been corrected utilizing audio tapes of the trial.

Many of Darlie's supporters feel that the transcript errors alone warrant a retrial.

However, it does not matter if the court stenographer typed out the entire novel of War and Peace during the trial, the jury still heard and seen the evidence against Darlie.

And the words typed in the record do not change that fact.

If a retrial were somehow granted it still wouldn't change the forensic evidence that convicted her.

In 1999, Judge Francis appoints court reporter Susan Simmons to recreate the trial transcripts from the original trial reporter Sandra Halsey's tapes.

Because Ms. Simmons had not attended the trial, she refuses to certify the new transcript once she completes it.

Judge Francis approves the new transcript without Ms. Simmons' certification.

The following year The Texas Court of Criminal Appeals overrules Darlie's objections to the corrected court reporter's record.

This forced Darlie's appeal to go forward with an uncertified and uncertain record of the trial.

The record of the trial would only be necessary if someone's direct testimony would be in question.

However, Darlie's case and conviction are based mainly on the physical evidence and the DNA at the crime scene which is not affected by the court reporter's transcripts.

Over the years DNA evidence has been tested. In the summer of 2015 DNA testing results were sealed and kept from the public's view.

The DNA results would have been given to both the prosecutor's office and Darlie's attorneys.

If the DNA results were in Darlie's favor we would have heard that by now.

The fact that no one is running around yelling that the DNA proves that someone else was in the Routier's home that night, and then the results don't show that.

I find it interesting that after the 2015 DNA results came back and were sealed, Darlie has refused requests for interviews.

As of 2021, Darlie's appeal is still being worked on by her attorney's and the prosecutor's office.

The state of Texas allows three appeals for a retrial.

As of 2021, Darlie has lost her direct appeal to the state and she lost her writ appeal to the state.

Her third appeal has been sent to the federal level with the U.S. District Court in San Antonio.

More DNA testing occurred in 2018.

From looking at the court record online we know that the federal court judge has not yet ruled on those DNA results.

If the judge denies further motions from Darlie's attorney, then that court will go ahead and set a date for the execution.

Over the years many people have written letters to the Texas court on Darlie's behalf.

Some of these are right out ridiculous and you can tell that the author of the letter never read any of the documents on the case.

Others claim that they know that Darlie is innocent. Despite all of the physical proof that she lied and made up the entire story of the events of that night.

One person who first claimed Darlie's guilt, but then changed her opinion, was book author Barbara Davis who wrote the book, *Precious Angels*.

I am not going to comment on a fellow author's opinion about a case that they write about.

But I will say that if she had a change of heart on Darlie's guilt, then why is her book *Precious Angels* still for sale?

I would think that the book would have been delisted and unpublished.

Many of Darlie's supports claim falsely that the book cannot be unpublished or that the books that are being sold are old used books that people are selling.

These statements are not true and the book is still being offered by the author through her publisher.

Timeline to Murder

If we take everything that has been shared online by Darlie's family and her supporters we would have to believe that this is what happened on the morning of June 6th.

A couple of inexperienced burglars are just cruising around the neighborhood in their black car looking for a house to rob.

They see the Routier's home all lit up with lights around the yard and their bright spotlights shining on a fountain right in front of the house.

They both realize that this is the best house to rob because the lights will help them in seeing what they are doing.

They drive down the back alley about 75 yards and park next to a garbage can while one of them gets out and takes a closer look in the Routier's back yard.

He struggles with the gate to get it to open up and he then notices the light from the television through the family room blinds.

He looks for an easy entry point into the house. And luckily for him, he finds windows that lead into the garage with screens on them.

But wait, he doesn't have anything on him to cut the screen. And the idea of just pulling the screen out of its frame doesn't come to mind; after all these burglars are inexperienced.

So he goes back out to the car and asks his partner if he has a knife so that he can cut the screen.

Sadly, his partner also left all of his burglary tools at home that night.

So after a short discussion, they decide to just go up to the door and ask to borrow a knife.

Luckily for them, this plan works fine. Darlie answers the door and the guy is given a bread knife with a promise that he will bring it back when he is done with it.

As he walks across the yard to the back yard he thinks to himself that he is lucky and doubts that she will even remember giving him the knife.

As his getaway driver waits patiently in the car, he slips back into the backyard and makes his way to the window closest to the house rather than choosing the one nearest to the gate.

He notices the sliding glass doors just a few feet to his right. He decides not to try and open them because he went to all of this work to get this bread knife, and damn it he was going to use it!

He cuts the window all the while praying that the window is unlocked and his purpose of borrowing the bread knife isn't all in vain.

He breathes a sigh of relief when he discovers that the window is unlocked. He thinks to himself that this must be his lucky night.

He climbs through the window and makes his way around the cat cage and the items that are piled along his path to the utility room door that leads into the house.

He slowly turns the knob and realizes that the door is unlocked.

He slips into the utility room and notices the light from the television is throwing a soft glow into the kitchen area.

He is happy because now he will be able to find the butcher block that the bread knife came from and return it as he promised.

He goes into the kitchen and returns the knife to the empty slot and looks around the kitchen.

A feeling of excitement overcomes him as he notices the jewelry and watch on the bar between the kitchen and the family room.

He slowly makes his way to the valuables on the counter and then in the glow of the television, he realizes that there are people asleep in the family room.

He thinks to himself, maybe I should try my hand at murder. This robbery crap is for the birds.

He creeps back through the kitchen and just as he is about to grab the largest butcher knife that he can find from the butcher block on the counter. He thinks to himself that he had better cover his hand so that he doesn't leave any fingerprints.

He goes back to the utility room and looks for the perfect hand covering. He is relieved to find a single sock.

He places the sock over his hand and heads back to the butcher block to retrieve the butcher knife.

He then heads toward the family room.

As he passes the wine rack his eyes automatically are drawn to the beautiful wine glasses that are in the glass holder.

Knowing that father's day is just ten days away he decides that his dad would just love a new wine glass.

He decides to take one of the glasses out of the holder and sets it on the shelf next to the ice bucket so that he can grab it on his way out the door.

He slowly enters the family room....passing the valuables on the countertop, to where the boys are sleeping in front of the TV.

He immediately stabs them. Devin is killed instantly but Damon is just severely wounded. But seeing this is the first murder he had ever committed he doesn't realize this yet.

He sees Darlie sleeping soundly on the couch. He thinks to himself how she looks just like an angel lying there sleeping; and how lucky he is that she is such a heavy sleeper and that she never woke up as he brutally stabbed the boys, just feet away from her.

He notices a small line of drool coming from the side of her mouth as she slept. He reaches down with the sock-covered hand and gently wipes the drool from her mouth; making sure not to get any of the small blood spots from the sock on her beautiful cheek.

He decides not to kill her.

After all, she was nice enough to let him borrow her bread knife and he couldn't kill a sweet woman like her.

He places the butcher knife into his back pocket and slowly makes his way out of the house the same way that he came in.

He gets back down the alley to the getaway car and just before climbing into the car he pulls the sock off his hand and throws it in the grass next to the garbage can. Making sure that it doesn't go into the drain and that it can be found easily. Just in case that sweet woman needs that sock and comes out looking for it.

His buddy asks excitedly, "So, what did you get?"

The killer's response was, "Nothing, but I did get a cool wine glass for my dad. Oh crap, I forgot my dad's wine glass. Hold on, I'll be right back"

He then gets back out of the car and heads back into the Routier's house the same way he went in the first time.

As he is climbing through the window this time he notices that he still has the butcher knife in his back pocket.

When he enters the kitchen, he goes over to the sink and rinses off the knife so that he doesn't leave any blood from the two boys on it.

He doesn't want to upset Darlie by leaving blood on her fancy knife.

Just then he realizes that Damon is still alive.

So he goes back into the family room and stabs the boy once again.

He now realizes that he needs to do something about the mother. She is going to remember him from when he came to barrow the bread knife earlier.

But he can see that she put a lot of time and money into her looks and he doesn't want to do anything so that the family couldn't have an open-casket funeral for such a beautiful woman.

So he slashes at Darlie so that he doesn't hit her in the face or puncture one of her fake breasts.

To his surprise, she wakes up and starts to fight him off.

She swings violently at him and he is doing all that he could to block her arms from hitting him and machining sure that the knife doesn't accidentally hit her face or breasts.

By the time he was able to get away; he had slashed her neck and cut her forearm.

He felt bad because he thought that he may have just attacked a deaf-mute woman. After all, she didn't hear the kids being attacked and she didn't scream out for help when they were fighting.

He heads out of the family room and makes his way to the utility room. He can see that she is getting up from the couch.

He then realizes that he needs to grab the wine glass that he had planned on giving to his dad.

As he is passing by the wine rack he reaches out to grab it. But in his rush to escape from Darlie, he drops the glass and it shatters all over the floor.

He says to himself, "Damn it, now I wish I would have at least stolen the watch on the counter."

As he ran out of the kitchen and into the utility room, he remembers that he has the woman's knife in his hand. And his conscience won't let him steal that poor woman's knife so he decides to drop it on the floor.

He goes out into the garage and is relieved to see that the woman isn't following him into the garage.

He still has father's day on his mind so he decides to go back into the house and get his dad the watch from the bar.

He opens the door and watches as Darlie is checking Damon, who followed her into the kitchen, for any wounds.

He then sees Darlie run down the hallway towards the front door yelling for somebody named Darin.

As she is down the hallway he goes back into the kitchen to get the watch for his father.

He notices that Damon is still alive and now lying on the floor near the wall of the family room.

Luckily for him, Darlie picked up the knife and set it up on the counter near the watch and jewelry.

He quickly grabs the knife and stabs Damon again as he lay on the floor.

These stabs caused Darlie's blood that was on the knife, to be cast-off on the wall next to where Damon was lying, now dying.

Down the hall, he could hear a man's voice so he decides to just leave the house empty-handed.

He goes out through the utility room door into the garage.

He feels bad that he has left so much of the woman's blood all over the place.

So he takes his shirt and makes sure to wipe down any blood or fingerprints that he may have left on the door handle on the garage side of the utility room door.

He knows how hard blood is to clean up on window sills, so as he slips back out the cut screen, he is making sure not to leave any blood on the window sill.

He goes back out the gate and as a courtesy, he decides to lift the gate off the ground and close it behind him.

He quickly goes down the alley to where his partner is waiting in the getaway car.

He jumps in the car and tells him, "Let's get out of here."

His partner says, "So did you get the wine glass?"

He replies, "No. I dropped it and it broke, so I got the hell out of there."

Man, that sucks, "His buddy replied."

"Well I almost got my dad a watch, but one of the boys was still alive so I had to stab him again and get out of there."

His partner replies, "Well, maybe next time."

As they drive off down the alley the killer tells the driver all about his luck and together they make plans to head to the casino.

Seeing that Darlie forgot most of the facts of the case in the weeks and months to follow the crime, they do become two of the luckiest criminals alive.

This version of the crime may seem like a fantasy.

But for Darlie's version of events (that she claims that she can remember) to be true, then this story is plausible.

For those who don't believe that this story is plausible, here is the timeline of events based on the physical evidence, trial testimony, autopsy reports, and the 911 call.

The times in our timeline are suggested times only. (Except for the documented times during the 911 call)

Just after midnight, Darin and Darlie would have been having their discussion when, according to Darin, Darlie asked for a divorce.

I truly believe that it was at this point the events of that night began.

Here is a diagram of where everyone was located when Darin went upstairs to go to bed.

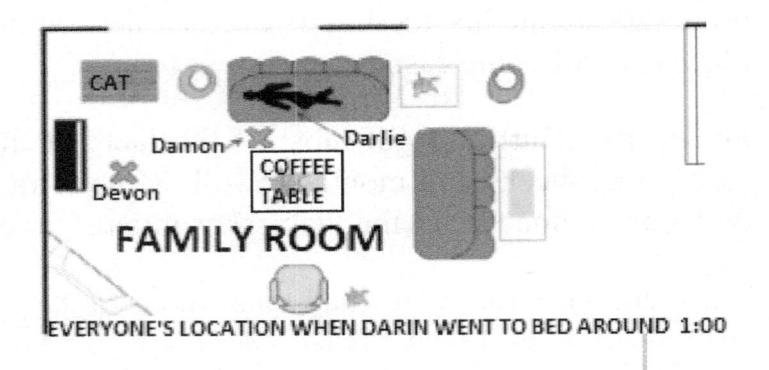

[Diagram: Family room layout showing CAT, Damon, Devon, COFFEE TABLE, Darlie positions]

EVERYONE'S LOCATION WHEN DARIN WENT TO BED AROUND 1:00

At approximately 1:00 a.m. Darin goes to bed.

Darlie's statement to the police: *Darin and I laid together for a little while and then decided to go to sleep because he had work the next day, this was around 12:30 or 1:00, I'm not sure.*

He kissed me and said he loved me, and I told him I loved him and would see him in the morning.

Darin's statement to the police: *We talked a little more about her going to Cancun with some friends across the street and I gave her a kiss goodnight.*

Told her to dream about me and went upstairs around 1:00 a.m.

Between 1:00 – 2:00 a.m.

Everyone in the house is either already asleep or close to being asleep, except for Darlie.

During this time she revisits photos of herself and the two boys in a photo album.

The investigators found the photo album open, and blood deposited on these pictures during the attacks.

I believe that Darlie's motive was to stage the crime scene to make it look like an intruder came in at this time.

Before 2:00 a.m.

Darlie takes the bread knife that would have been with the recently washed dishes on the counter and goes into the garage and cuts the screen.

As she exits the garage and enters into the utility room she picks up a sock to put over her hand to try and hide her fingerprints on the murder weapon that she is going to get next.

When she returns to the kitchen she places the bread knife into the butcher block.

We know that this was most likely done before either one of the boys being stabbed as there is no blood at all located inside of the garage.

Some people say that the screen could have been cut after both of the boys were stabbed the first time and when she returned from dropping the sock down the alley and before stabbing Damon the second time.

And to explain the lack of blood they say that she could have been holding a towel to her neck wound at that time.

I doubt this theory as the police did not find any traces of blood on the bread knife. If she had already stabbed the boys and cut herself, I would think that blood would have gotten on the bread knife somewhere.

And the time that Damon dies from his injuries suggests that this was done before his second attack.

We will use the police department's blood map to detail the stabbings of the two boys.

✪ Devon	◆ Damon	Ⓜ Darlie
✪M Devon & Darlie	Ⓜ◆ Damon & Darlie	M-3 Devon, Damon & Darlie

Devon's blood location is marked with a circle with a star.

Damon is marked with a circle and a diamond.

Darlie's blood location is marked with a circle with a letter "M". (as she is the main contributor of the blood at the scene)

And where the police found mixtures of Darlie's blood it is marked with a letter M and the diamond or star to determine which son her blood was mixed with.

At the sink, Darlie's blood was found mixed with both boys' blood.

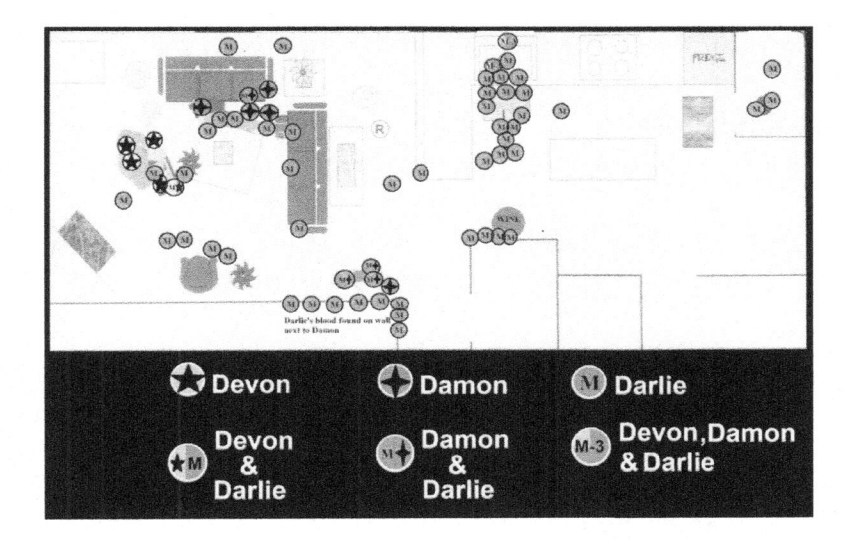

After Darlie puts the bread knife in the butcher block, she puts the sock over her hand and takes the largest butcher knife from the block.

At approximately 2:00 a.m.

We cannot tell if Devon or Damon was stabbed first.

Many believe that Devon was stabbed first and that Damon was awakened while Darlie was stabbing Devon.

Devon's autopsy report lists four wounds.

Three were described as stab wounds and one was described as an incised wound /cut.

Wounds #1 & 2 are both stab wounds to the chest.

Wound #3 is an incised wound /cut to his left forearm about 2 ¾ inches up from his wrist.

And finally, wound #4 is a stab wound to his posterior left thigh (thigh).

We are going to look at Darin's testimony here for a second.

Question, "What did you see when you went into the Roman room?"

Answer, "Devon laying on the floor."

Question, "Okay. Now we have seen certain photographs where Devon's body is over across the

Roman room, close to the big screen television, is that where you saw his body?"

Answer, "Yes, sir."

Question, "Was he still face up when you were over there to look at him?"

Answer, "Yes, sir."

Question, "What was his condition when you saw him?"

Answer, "Lifeless, two wounds in his chest, eyes open, looking up at me, no movement."

This photo shows where Devon's blood was found by the police.

As you can see, there is very little movement from where Devon was stabbed and where his body was discovered and all of the blood location.

You will also notice that there was blood that was tested in that area that was a mixture of Devin and Darlie's blood.

★ Devon

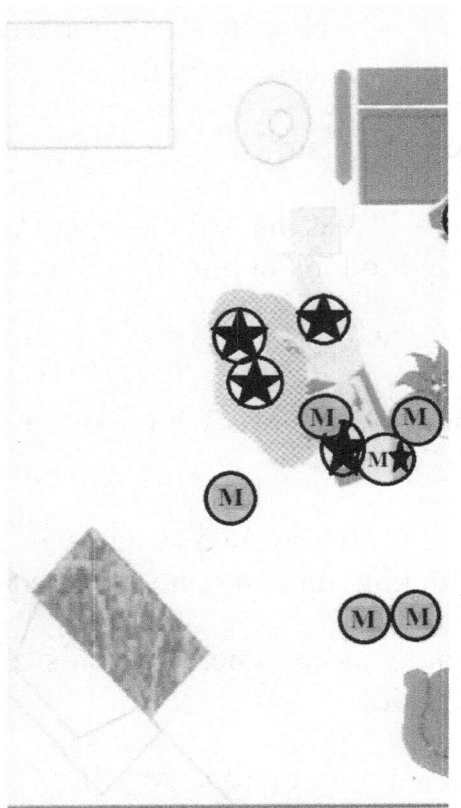

Ⓜ Devon & Darlie

Many people say because Devon was lying face-up on the floor and lifeless then we know that the stabs to his chest were the final blows.

I doubt this theory. Because if he had been stabbed in the thigh, then I believe that he would have screamed out in pain and awakened his father upstairs.

I believe that he was stabbed both times in the upper chest before the wound to his thigh.

The first stab in the left side of his chest perforated the upper left lobe of the lung, the pulmonary artery of the heart, and the lower right lobe of the lung.

This stab came from left to right.

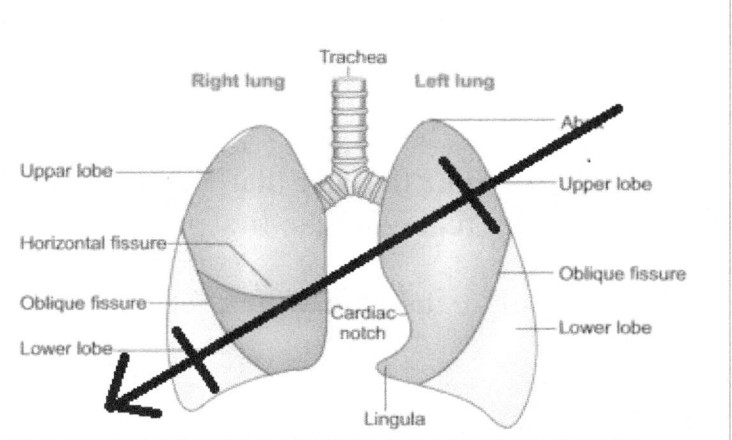

DEVON'S KNIFE WOUND PATH FROM THE LEFT UPPER LOBE TO THE RIGHT LOWER LOBE

I believe that this wound passing through both lungs made it impossible for him to scream out for help.

After the first stab wound, he may have rolled over and tried to get away from Darlie or lifted his legs to kick her away, and that would be how he received the stab wound to his thigh.

Once she was able to get him flat on his back he may have tried to block the knife from stabbing him again and that would cause the cut to his left forearm about 2 ¾ inches up from his wrist.

Once he was on his back again Darlie would deliver the final blow to his chest and penetrating his liver.

This stab wound came from the right to the left, which tells us that the attacker was in a different position than when the first stab to the chest was delivered.

This would support the fact that Devon fought off his mother after receiving the first stab.

And this would cause the wound to his thigh and forearm.

And if Devin was kicking at his mother's arms to get her away from him that would explain how she could have received the bruising on her forearms.

However, her supporters claim that Devin kicking for his life would not be strong enough to bruise Darlie's arms.

Devon would have bled to death pretty quickly from his wounds.

I believe that it was during this attack that Damon was woken up.

At approximately 2:07 – 2:08 a.m.

Darlie then stabs Damon next to the couch area in the living room.

Devon has died of his wounds by this time.

She believes that both of the boys are now dead so she decides to clean off the knife and plant the sock with the boy's blood on it, down the back alley to make the police think that the killer fled that direction.

All of the boy's major injuries were internal. And this would be why there was not a lot of blood on the knife from either boy.

Darlie goes to the sink and washes off the knife.

This explains how both Devon and Damon's blood mixed with Darlie's is located at the sink.

At approximately 2:10 a.m.

Darlie sits on the trunk by the front door and puts on the high tops. She exits the house through the front door and drops the sock 75 yards down the alley next to the garbage can where it can be found.

Her goal is not to dispose of the sock because there was a sewer drain right in front of the Routier's house if that was her intention.

At approximately 2:18 a.m.

Darlie returns to the house, where she slips her feet out of the still laced high-tops.

At approximately 2:19 a.m.

She stands at the kitchen sink and cuts her neck and arm.

She is bleeding pretty well from her self-inflicted wounds and attempts to clean up the blood around the sink area. She uses only one side of the sink as the baby bottle is still upright in the other.

She then goes to the utility room to double-check that she unlocked the back door leading to the garage so that she can explain the exit route to the police.

While in the utility room she drips blood on the floor in the area where she never stated to the police that she went.

She leaves her blood on the door and the side of the Washing machine

She then realizes that Damon is not dead and has made his way to the end of the hallway across from the bathroom door.

Many people believe that during this time Damon tried to stand by using the glass top table leaving his print in Darlie's blood.

During the trial, it was believed to have come from Damon. Because of the size of the ridge detail, it is believed the print belonged to a juvenile or possibly a five- or six-year-old child.

And we know that Devon never moved from where he was stabbed.

At approximately 2:29 a.m.

Darlie stabs Damon a second time next to the wall at the end of the hallway in the living room.

Her blood is cast-off as she swings the knife down into Damon's back.

She then goes over to Devon to make sure that he is dead.

She places the knife on the floor leaving an imprint of her blood on the carpet from where it ran down her arm from her forearm cut to the knife's point.

She tips the glass tabletop over and leaves drops of her blood on the top of the glass tabletop in a downward drip pattern before she tips it on its side.

After tipping the glass top she walks along the front of the couches and places the knife on the counter between the kitchen and the living room.

At approximately 2:30 a.m.

She goes to the wine rack where she grabs a single wineglass and smashes it on the kitchen floor and screams for Darin and he immediately comes downstairs.

At exactly 2:31 a.m.

Darlie calls 911 started at 2:31 a.m. and lasted five minutes and forty-four seconds.

At exactly **2:34:54 am:**

The voice of Officer David Waddell, the first police officer who arrived on the scene is heard on the 911 recording, telling Darlie to "lay down . . . ok. . . just sit down." Darlie tells Waddell "they ran out in the garage."

At this point, Damon is still alive. (Stabbed 5 minutes earlier)

At approximately 2:37 am: Time estimated by Sgt. Walling's written report.

The second officer, Sergeant Walling, arrives at the Routier's house at the same time as the ambulance.

At this point, Damon is still alive. (Stabbed 7-8 minutes earlier)

At approximately 2:38- 2:39 a.m., the paramedics enter the house

During the trial paramedic, Brian Koschak was asked when they entered the house.

Question, "Okay. Did you and Paramedic Kolbye immediately get out of the ambulance and go inside the house?"

Answer, "Not immediately, no, sir."

Question, "Did you wait for Sergeant Walling to clear the house for you?"

Answer, "Yes, sir."

Question, "Do you know about what -- how much time it took for Sergeant Walling to clear the house before you and Paramedic Kolbye would be allowed inside?"

Answer, "One to two minutes."

So, based on Sergeant Walling's estimated arrival time of 2:37, Paramedics Brian Koschak and Paramedic Jack Kolbye enter the house at about 2:38- 2:39 a.m.

Damon is barely alive. (Stabbed approximately 8-9 minutes earlier)

Here is the testimony of Paramedic jack Kolbye who was at the Routier's house and tried to save Damon's life.

Question "All right. Where did you go in the room?"

Answer "As soon as I entered the room, I looked at Officer Waddell, he gave me a nod indicating a direction that I looked in, and there I saw a small child laying on the floor."

Question "Okay. Where was he in the room?"

Answer "Just to my left as I walked in."

Question "Okay. So you just go into the family room and he's right there on your left; is that right?"

Answer "That's correct."

Question "How was he positioned? Was he on the floor?"

Answer "He was lying face down on the floor."

Question "And what did you do?"

Answer "I walked over to the child and examined his backside briefly for any injuries, and I rolled him over."

Question "Do you recall how he was clothed?"

Answer "He had on a dark T-shirt and blue jeans."

Question "You say then that you examined his back. Let me ask you: Was there any kind of a rag or towel or anything else on top of that child?"

Answer "No, there was not."

Question "Are you sure about that?"

Answer "I'm absolutely sure about that."

Question "Okay. He's got on blue jeans and he's got on a black shirt. Right?"

Answer "That's correct."

Question "You say that you turned him over; is that right?"

Answer "I rolled him over, yes, sir."

Question "Okay. And what, if anything, occurred when you rolled the child over?"

Answer "He gasped for a gasp of air, and that was the final time that he breathed."

At approximately 2:39-2:40 a.m. Damon took his last breath of air

(Stabbed approximately 9 minutes earlier)

At approximately 2:40 2:41 a.m.

Damon is taken out to the ambulance.

The paramedic testifies that Damon was dead when he moved him out to the ambulance.

Question "Okay. What was his condition, at the time that you started to move him out to the ambulance?"

Answer "He was not breathing. There was no pulse."

We do know that *Damon* was *alive* when the paramedics arrived on the scene and the medical examiner testified that he could only have survived approximately eight to nine minutes after receiving his fatal stab wounds.

Darlie's supporters claim that the timeline is impossible.

They keep repeating that the state's expert testified that Damon, who was still alive when the paramedics arrived, could not have lived any longer than 9 minutes.

They focus on the fact that the 911 call lasts for five minutes and forty-four seconds.

They point out that Darlie is on the phone the entire time so she could not have stabbed Damon during that time.

They even point out that the paramedics were held up for one to two minutes by the police officers that were inside clearing the house before they allowed them in to try and save the boys.

They falsely claim that this only gives Darlie approximately 1 minute and 16 seconds to inflict her wounds, stage a crime scene, and plant the bloody sock 75 yards down the back alley from the Routier home.

Sadly all of the supporters are wrong and Darlie did have the time to stab the boys, plant the sock, inflict her wounds, stage a crime scene, and stab Damon a second time before calling 911.

And our time frame proves that.

In Closing

It has been over 20 years since Damon and Devon were brutally murdered in their home by their mother Darlie.

Darlie Routier still sits on death row, one of only six women, waiting out the results of her final appeal.

In June 2011, Darin and Darlie divorced.

Darin said that the decision was mutual and "very difficult," and that he still believes that Darlie is innocent.

Darin also said that they decided to divorce to end the "limbo" that they had been in since her arrest in 1996 and conviction the following year.

Many people say that Darin may have had a hand in the deaths of the two boys.

Some have even asked as to why Darlie has never named him as a codefendant in the case.

It is because the day that she admits that she did kill her sons. The appeals all come to an end and her death warrant is signed by the Governor of Texas.

Her case has been a journey of appeals and DNA testing. And to this day, nothing has pointed to anyone else killing her boys but her.

In 2019, Dallas County Judge Gracie Lewis issued an order for the Texas Department of Criminal Justice to utilize the FBI's Automated Fingerprint Identification System to find the person who left the print on the glass tabletop.

In the first week of 2020, a joint status report filed by Darlie's defense team and the state of Texas with the U.S. Court of Appeals in West Texas said the images of the prints were run, but no match was obtained.

One of Darlie's attorneys, J. Stephen Cooper of Dallas, said that the story of the unidentified prints will not end there.

Cooper also said, testing of DNA evidence obtained from articles of clothing found during the investigation has been completed but said the defense is hoping additional DNA testing will be done.

And for the 1st time, the Dallas County district attorney has permitted the defense to inspect its files on Darlie's case.

Darlie's federal appeal has been put on hold pending the outcome of hearings at the state level.

In 2021 the case is still moving along with more DNA tests. And once the results are back, and they don't point to anyone else besides Darlie as the killer, then she will be given a date for the execution.

Sadly too many people claim that Darlie just couldn't have killed her two boys.

They have written letters to the judge hoping that in some way they could sway the judge to see Darlie through their eyes.

What they fail to realize is that the judge doesn't even read the letters. They just get filed away with the rest of the letters sent on Darlie's behalf.

But thankfully, the judge has to see Darlie through the eyes of the law. And no matter what anybody writes, the physical evidence and Darlie's account of what happened that night screams that she is 100% guilty.

Some say that she couldn't do it because she was a mother who loved her kids.

But they forget about the mothers who did kill their kids.

Susan Smith, who killed her two sons, 14-month-old Alex and 3-year-old Michael, in October 1994.

And those who knew her said that she loved her kids.

But Darlie's supporters say that Darlie couldn't do it because she was a mother who loved her kids.

And then we have Marybeth Tinning, who killed nine of her children between 1972 and 1985. And those who knew her said that she loved her kids.

But Darlie's supporters say that Darlie couldn't do it because she was a mother who loved her kids.

In 1983, Diane Downs' three children were brought to an Oregon hospital with gunshot wounds. One died, and two survived but had serious injuries. And those who knew her said that she loved her kids.

But Darlie's supporters say that Darlie couldn't do it because she was a mother who loved her kids.

And let's not forget, in 2001, another Texas mom Andrea Yates killed her five children, who ranged in age from 6 months to 7 years old, in a bathtub. And those who knew her said that she loved her kids.

But yet again, Darlie's supporters say that Darlie couldn't do it because she was a mother who loved her kids.

On January 31, 1997, Greg Davis said it best in his closing statement.

Only God and she knows exactly why she did it. But we have a pretty darn good idea, don't we, of the kind of pressure that was building up that night on June 6th of 1996.

You know these two children here, well, they lived in Rowlett and I never had the pleasure of meeting them, but you know, once upon a time, they were ours too.

They weren't just Darlie Routier's children, they were ours.

You see, they were our neighborhood kids too. The kids we saw running up and down the streets on their bicycles. They were our classmates. They were our students. These children right here.

In a real sense, they were our future.

You know, and as these two precious children, laid on that carpet, looking up with those opened eyes, literally drowning in their own blood as they laid on that carpet, as Mr. Shook said to you, the very last thing that each of these two children saw was their killer.

Can you imagine what it must have been like for those two children that morning as they saw this woman right here?

THE DEFENDANT: Liar, liar.

MR. GREG DAVIS: She says liar now --

THE DEFENDANT: You are a liar.

MR. GREG DAVIS: See. See. But --

THE DEFENDANT: I did not kill my kids.

MR. GREG DAVIS: But they looked up there, and they saw this woman right here, in a rage, coming down on them with that knife, and that is the very last thing that they saw. They saw their killer, and after these four weeks, you have seen her too.

Her name is Darlie Lynn Routier.

Made in the USA
Coppell, TX
07 November 2021